AUSTERLITZ
1805

AUSTERLITZ
1805

CHRISTOPHER DUFFY

ARCHON BOOKS

First published in Great Britain 1977 by
Leo Cooper Ltd,
196 Shaftesbury Avenue, London WC2H 8JL
and in the United States of America by
Archon Books
an imprint of The Shoe String Press, Inc.,
Hamden, Connecticut

ISBN 0–208–01702–X

Printed in Great Britain

CONTENTS

ILLUSTRATIONS

*The author and publishers are grateful to the following for permission to repro-
duce copyright illustrations: Dr Paddy Griffith, no 15; The British Library,
nos 3, 6, 7, 8, 9, 10 and 11.*

MAPS

Drawn by the Author

INTRODUCTION

The Battle of Austerlitz was the first, and some would say the greatest victory of Napoleon's *Grande Armée*. This episode considerably helped Napoleon to extend his power over Europe, and thus enabled him to establish a recognizable continental community a century and a half before the Common Market (or so The Ogre's apologists would like us to think). Apart from its historical significance the battle possesses great narrative and human interest, which for most of us stems from the graphic re-creation of that day in Tolstoy's *War and Peace*, through which millions have come to know the main features of the action, and the characters of some of the chief participants—people like the wily old General Kutuzov, or the weak and impressionable Tsar Alexander.

What has been lacking up to now has been a comprehensive treatment of this dramatic theme. Previous studies have treated the campaign of 1805 and its final battle as a text-book example of Napoleonic warfare, whilst disregarding the viewpoint of the Russians and Austrians, who managed to get themselves so badly beaten. However it is both possible and necessary to look at the other side of the hill, now that the Russians have published the correspondence of Kutuzov and his generals. Many further details can be supplied from the very informative material in the Austrian war archives, and the unpublished reports of the horrified British observers. Incidents like the attack of the Russian

Imperial Guard at Austerlitz can be interpreted in a new light, when we view them with the help of a more comprehensive documentation.

I hope that *Austerlitz 1805* will present a more balanced assessment of the battle than any other available study. At the same time I renounce any claim to have produced a definitive account of this very complicated action. One of the survivors of Austerlitz, Lieutenant-Colonel Ermolov, has some wise words on the subject:

> 'I have had occasion to hear many able officers debating the battle, but not a single one of them had a clear understanding of what had happened. They could only agree that they had seen no event to match it. Posterity will no doubt give birth to various studies of the battle. It will, however, be difficult to repose complete confidence in them—it is easy enough to put together an account of individual episodes, but not so easy to establish the relationship between them, or to match events and times.'

You will find that criticism of commanders in this book is on the whole less emphatic than is the fashion in much contemporary military history. In my own map-reading and drill I was aptly described by a Sandhurst CSM as being as much use as 'an ashtray on a motor bike'. I also harbour memories of a scene beside the Danube in 1971, when I helped to push and pull a mutinous rabble of Yugoslav territorials into a reconstruction of the march over the Pratzen, later to be shown on the BBC TV serial of *War and Peace*. It remains a source of wonder to me that generals get their forces to a field in the first place, let alone do anything constructive with them when they have arrived.

Names of people and places are rendered with an eye to familiarity rather than absolute consistency. Nobody could reasonably be expected to make sense of a general who spelled his name 'Przebyszewski'. Using one of the contemporary Russian pronunciations I have therefore taken the liberty of calling him 'Prebyshevsky'.

I owe a great deal to the patient help of the staff of the *Kriegsarchiv*, Vienna. I also wish to thank the staffs of the Public Record Office, the London Library, the Army Department Library, and the Central Library of the RMA Sandhurst. Brigadier Peter Young and Colonel John Elting assisted with further material and references.

In particular I am grateful for the expertise and support of David Chandler, Dr Richard Holmes and Dr Paddy Griffith, who accompanied me on a visit to the field of Austerlitz. I dedicate this book to them, and to the unfailingly cheerful Czechs whom we encountered on our expedition.

'The Emperor Napoleon's most famous victory.'

BERTHIER TO TALLEYRAND ON THE FIELD OF AUSTERLITZ

'So far God has kept me safe and well, though I have already been in frightful battles and seen comrades killed at my side. But I hope to see you again in the same good state as when I left you. My dearest mother, we must be brave. It is God's will, and we should not despair. With the grace of God we shall meet again . . .'

LETTER OF TROOPER JEAN–BAPTISTE REFELD, KILLED AT AUSTERLITZ, 2 DECEMBER, 1805

CHAPTER 1

THE THREE EMPERORS

MOST people have formed their own vision of Napoleon Bonaparte, if only from the strutting little man of the brandy advertisements, with the vast black hat, and one hand stuck inside the lapels of his coat. More pompously, military pundits from Clausewitz onwards have acclaimed Napoleon as the 'god of war', while historians regard him as one of the forces which propelled Europe into the modern age.

In most of us there is enough of the romantic to respond to the story of the diminutive Corsican gunner who set Europe by the ears, and who could address the Emperor of Austria (without too much presumption) as *Monsieur mon Frère*. As Kenneth Clark has indicated, there are traits about the man which are

> 'painfully reminiscent of Hitler and Wagner. And yet one can't quite resist the exhilaration of Napoleon's glory. Communal enthusiasms may be a dangerous intoxicant; but if human beings were to lose altogether the sense of glory, I think we should be the poorer, and when religion is in decline it is an alternative to naked materialism.'[1]

In the first years of the nineteenth century we encounter Napoleon in one of his more constructive moods, when he was concerned to re-establish in France an order that could be respected by men of sense and taste. The nation had been wearied by a decade of war, and by the incompetence of the Directory—

1

the lacklustre committee which had mismanaged the French Republic in the later 1790s. The people were, therefore, ready to admire a decisive soldier like Napoleon, who could wage war speedily and cheaply, and help to force the enemies of France to the conference table. Austria came to terms at Lunéville in February, 1801, and Russia, Naples, Portugal and Turkey queued up to make their accommodations as well. Britain too was prevailed upon to sign a treaty of peace, at Amiens in March, 1802.

Napoleon could now strive for something more: to invest himself with the full authority that was due to the leader of the French nation. Already First Consul, he persuaded the people to vote him Consul for Life in 1802, and on 2 December, 1804, he crowned himself Emperor of the French in Nôtre Dame Cathedral.

The new France was already well advanced on the way of consolidation. Napoleon reorganized education, reformed the law, revived flagging industries, built new roads and repaired the old ones. After all the turmoils and absurdities of the Revolution, the nation as a whole welcomed the settlement which Napoleon reached with the Catholic Church. The clergy now put their moral authority behind the régime, and supporters of the old Bourbon royal family began to wonder whether they ought to adapt themselves to the new order in France. In 1805 Napoleon made bold to abolish the Republican Calendar, 'one of the most stupid inventions of the Revolution',[2] and in the same year he gave further evidence of his sound judgment when he decreed: 'Horse races shall be established successively in the departments of the Empire most notable for the quality of horses which are bred there. Prizes shall be awarded to the swiftest animals.'[3]

In all his proceedings Napoleon was aware that 'people in general, and the French above all, love to be dazzled by ostentation and high-flown titles'.[4] Deserving public servants were admitted to the Legion of Honour, or to one of the grandly-named offices of the new Imperial court, while the great generals vied with one another for the distinction of the marshalate, which brought almost princely honours.

The parvenu Empire stood very much upon its dignity, and

2

Napoleon frowned upon those ministers who clung to the free and easy habits of the Directory, such as accompanying prostitutes to the public theatre. There was an embarrassing scene when Tsar Alexander of Russia tried to show his good will towards two of Napoleon's emissaries, by addressing them in the old Republican style—'this was not at all to the taste of Bonaparte's two envoys, who had to make repeated protest that it was not the custom of France to call people by the name "citizen". '5

Whatever his work of reconciliation at home, Napoleon was clearly unable to accept the old order of things in Europe. In almost every way he affronted the former partners of the Second Coalition. The makeshift peace with England broke apart in the summer of 1803. The British imposed a blockade on the French coast, while Napoleon in his turn closed all the ports under his control to British commerce, and assembled an army of invasion in the famous Camp of Boulogne.

In Germany Napoleon pressed home the initiative he had gained over the Austrians, and made secondary states like Bavaria and Württemberg into his clients and potential allies. In Italy too he embarked on a series of provocations, culminating in the virtual annexation of a large part of the north in 1805.

To the liberal-minded elements in Europe it was only too clear that Napoleon had arrayed himself in the ranks of 'ambitious men and sovereigns of the ordinary kind'.6 The Romantics' disillusionment was shared to the full by the pale and impressionable Tsar Alexander of Russia. This amiable young gentleman (he was only twenty-eight at the time of Austerlitz) had come to the throne in appalling circumstances in 1801, when his father Paul I was murdered by a group of courtiers. Alexander was consumed by praiseworthy ambitions, and one of Napoleon's staff had to admit that: 'Nature had done a great deal for him, and it would have been difficult to find a model of greater perfection and grace . . . however Tsar Alexander was already afflicted with a slight deafness on the left side, and he inclined his right ear to listen to what was being said to him . . . he spoke the French language in all its purity, without trace of foreign accent, and he made a constant use of its fine academic phrases.'7 At the same time there was something unstable, something almost feminine in the Tsar's character, 'with all the attendant consequences, whether attractive, good or annoying. In his imagination he often conceived projects which were pleasing enough to him, but could not be reconciled with reality.'[8]

Alexander had greeted the coming of Napoleon with genial curiosity. However, it was entirely characteristic that he should now suddenly discover in Napoleon the chief threat to Europe's welfare and happiness, which stood under the protection of Russia. What distressed Alexander chiefly was the lawless manner in which Napoleon had kidnapped the Duke of Enghien from neutral German territory, and had him shot for his supposed involvement in a conspiracy. Alexander accordingly approached Britain and Austria with a view to reviving the anti-French coalition.

Many of the Austrians doubted the wisdom of renewing this alliance. As sovereign of a ramshackle congeries of provinces, Emperor Francis II hesitated to give way to the promptings of the Russians and English, and people like his own cabinet minister Count Colloredo, who urged that only a new alliance could save Austria from the boundless ambitions of Napoleon. The Emperor's reluctance was shared by his brother the Archduke Charles, an experienced soldier and strategist, who pointed out that Russia was an untrustworthy ally, and that the history of the last hundred and fifty years indicated that Britain was unlikely to risk a powerful land force on the Continent: 'Apart from Marlborough, no Englishman has believed that Britain could strive for the dominion of the seas by fighting on the Danube.'[9]

Emperor Francis himself remains a shadowy figure throughout our tale. He was less than ten years Alexander's senior yet his battered and sagging appearance made him seem infinitely older. In the course of time Francis' intelligence and sense of duty earned him his subjects' respect, but in the year of Austerlitz he exercised little discernible influence over the course of affairs. The Austrians had signed a vague preliminary treaty with the Russians on 4 November, 1804, with the unexpressed hope that Alexander would now leave them in peace. With this encouragement the Tsar approached the British, and on 11 April, 1805, the representatives of Alexander and King George agreed on the fundamentals of a

4

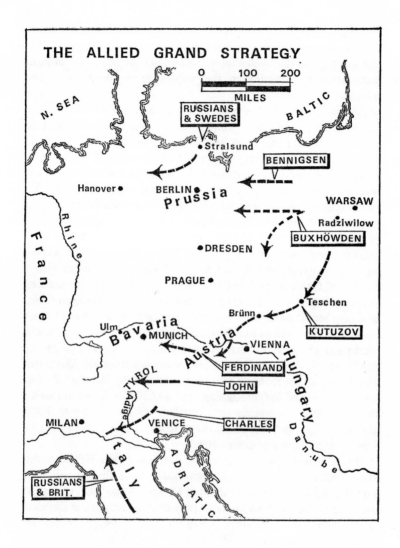

THE ALLIED GRAND STRATEGY

new coalition, which would throw back the French to their old boundaries.

Francis allowed events to overtake him. The Austrians tamely accepted the *fait accompli* of the Anglo-Russian treaty, and on 16 July they agreed on a detailed military convention with the

5

Russians, virtually committing themselves to the nascent coalition. Eventually, on 9 August, Austria made its formal accession to the union, and declared that it would 'set its forces in motion without delay, trusting in the loyalty of its partners to the alliance'.[10]

Alexander and his entourage had already settled on the outlines of the Third Coalition's grand strategy, but it was the sort of plan that might come from an overhasty perusal of a small scale map, or the rapid twirling of a globe of the world.

The combined forces were to take the offensive on a vast front stretching from the Baltic to the southern Mediterranean. The main Russian effort was to be directed towards northern and central Germany, with General Bennigsen making ready to move through Prussia with 40,000 men, and General Kutuzov with 50,000 troops marching south-west to the Danube or wherever else the Austrians wanted him to go. General Buxhöwden with a further 50,000 was to lend help in either direction as circumstances arose: to begin with he was to support Bennigsen's southern flank, and help him to put pressure on the Prussians; then he would most likely peel off south to join Kutuzov and the Austrians somewhere along the Danube. Further Austrian forces were to operate in the Tyrol and northern Italy. Almost as an afterthought Alexander calculated on throwing in two diversions on the strategic flanks. A mixed force of 20,000 Russians and 16,000 Swedes would strike from Swedish Pomerania into northern Germany, while 9,000 British troops and 25,000 Russians from Corfu were to land in Naples and liberate southern Italy.

It was hoped that the Bavarians, the Saxons, the Hessians, the Brunswickers and the Danes would join the advancing columns, and that King Frederick William of Prussia would yield to reason and threats, and put his immaculately-drilled army at the disposal of the alliance. Altogether Alexander reckoned on setting in motion a host of at least 500,000 men.

The whole scheme was shot through with Alexander's sense of messianic mission. He instructed General Kutuzov to declare to the peoples of western Europe that the Russians intended to make no conquests for themselves, nor to deprive any nation of the freedoms it had acquired in recent years, but solely to restore the peace and independence of states. He was confident that the populations of France, Switzerland and Italy would prove sympathetic to his cause, as soon as they were appraised of 'the real reasons why we were impelled into the war'.[11]

CHAPTER 2

THE *GRANDE ARMÉE*

As the eighteenth century wore on, there were signs that military men were becoming impatient with the measured and restrained proceedings of conventional warfare. An Austrian field-marshal, the Prince de Ligne, urged that one should show humanity to an enemy only after he had been convincingly beaten: 'There should be nothing agreeable about warfare. God forbid that I should recommend brutality, but we must face facts like men. It is not a trade for a philosopher.'[1]

For a variety of reasons the French became the first practitioners of a more vigorous and decisive mode of combat. To begin with a number of the officers of the old royal army had been at work on the mechanics of the military art. On the strategic level Bourcet and Broglie had investigated the means of breaking down the army into handier, self-contained formations which would enable the commander to exploit all the opportunities offered by terrain and circumstance. On the tactical side, the experts had thrashed out some eminently practical evolutions which combined the fire-power of formations in line with the manœuvrability of formations in column. Moreover, some important technological advances were incorporated in the light, standardized and mass-produced weapons such as the range of artillery introduced by Jean-Baptiste de Gribeauval, or the 'Charleville' musket of 1777. All of these achievements survived the turmoil of the Revolution.

Shortly after the battle of Austerlitz a British major frankly avowed:

'I have always considered the superiority of the French troops over those of the Continent, as the result of their individual intelligence; arising in a great degree from the habit of every Frenchman, to discuss whatever topic comes under his notice . . . Let us hear no more then of soldiers being mere machines. The absurdity of the doctrine is too palpable to need refutation.'[2]

This touched on one of the most important legacies of the Revolution. At first sight there was little in the French mass armies which terrorized Europe in the middle 1790s to appeal to the professional eye. However, these ragged conscripts were crusading for what they believed to be the advantage of mankind, as interpreted by their national leaders in Paris. Now at last commanders had troops who could be trusted to fight in dispersed formation out of the immediate sight of their officers, or to go foraging for themselves and return in the fullness of time to their units. For this reason, the soldiers of Revolutionary France outmatched the overdrilled troops of monarchical Europe, who fought according to rigid tactics, and whose movements were largely determined by the availability of magazines and supply trains.

For the first time something approaching the full human resources of a nation could be put at the disposal of a government at war. Not only were the ranks of the Revolutionary armies completed with conscripts, but the principle of a 'career open to talent' rendered the highest commands accessible to clever but coarse soldiers like Augereau and Masséna, who would not have been admitted to the polite society of superior officers under the *Ancien Régime*.

Old Europe was shaken to its foundations when Napoleon Bonaparte brought together the technical mastery of the Bourbon army with the moral achievement of the Revolution. By 1803, as First Consul for Life, he possessed the authority to weld the disparate elements of the old Revolutionary formations into the unique battle-winning institution which became known as the *Grande Armée*.

The nucleus of the new forces was created on the chalk downs around the Channel port of Boulogne. Napoleon's immediate objective was to gather a number of flotillas along the coast, and by a diversion to seize an opportunity to throw his army across the water and invade England. In late March, 1805, Admiral Villeneuve's squadron duly dodged out of the Mediterranean port of Toulon, and made for the West Indies in an attempt to draw the British warships from the Channel. Napoleon had already begun to embark the artillery and other heavy equipment for the invasion on the transports at Boulogne, and by June everything was on board except small arms, ammunition and other provisions.

According to Ségur, the fatal news reached Napoleon at four in the morning of 13 August that Villeneuve had returned from the West Indies, only to let himself be bottled up in the northern Spanish port of Ferrol. Thus the diversion had failed. For an hour Napoleon strode up and down swearing. 'His manner . . . was wild. His hat was jammed over his brows, and his eyes were blazing . . . "Do you know where that bloody fool Villeneuve has gone? He's at Ferrol! At Ferrol, for heaven's sake!" '[3]

For about a week now the Emperor had been concerned about the build-up of Austrian forces in Italy and central Europe, and after the tidings from Ferrol he made up his mind to turn his back on the Channel and march inland to attack the Austrians. The settling of accounts with the British would have to be postponed.

By this time Napoleon had accomplished such wonderful things with his forces at Boulogne that people began to speculate whether he had ever been serious about invading England, and whether the real purpose of the encampment had been to train up his new formations. Certainly we can now begin to speak for the first time of an entity called 'Napoleon's Army', or the *Grande Armée*, and so the course of events at Boulogne is of more than passing interest to us.

The term 'encampment' is something of a misnomer for the vast military town where many thousands of men dwelt for more than two years. 'Every regiment and company had its garden, lawns of verdant turf had been created as if by magic around the huts of the commanders and officers, which were designed with as much elegance as practicality.'[4] While the officers lived in some style, the men dug pits into the chalky soil to serve as their accommodation, and covered the top with timber and thatch. Makeshift abodes like these were comfortable enough in summer, but during the winter the sodden earth exuded streams of water through the holes made by mice and insects. One of the musicians came off parade to find the floor of his hut

'turned into a pond where pieces of clothing, sheets of music, bits of straw, love letters and forage caps were floating around instead of ducks and swans. We set to work at once with our canteens and mess tins to drain this untidy stretch of water. While we were thus engaged, the roof, being no longer supported at the sides, collapsed on our heads and filled our damp habitation with its wreckage.'[5]

The official rations consisted of three-quarters of a kilo of bread per day, some thin soup, and a few scraps of tough meat 'together with sinews, gristle and other culinary delights which the cooks, in their facetious way, liked to call their "special treat" '.[6]

This did little to assuage the men's hunger in the keen sea air, and the soldiers filled their stomachs with dandelion leaves, or whatever urchins or shellfish could be foraged from the sea shore. Napoleon's troops addressed themselves to this gastronomic beachcombing with as much thoroughness as French holiday-makers today. The artillery lieutenant Amand d'Hautpoul was walking across the sands at low tide when he came across a curious rock which was riven by a deep crevice. 'I was carrying a stick, and I put it into the hole to ascertain the depth. To my astonishment some powerful force drew it strongly inside. I called up a friend, who inserted his stick and experienced the same effect.' They drew out a large and vigorous octopus and brought it to their battery, 'where our gunners made it into a splendid meal'.[7]

If the 'storm-tossed ships' of the main British squadrons stood well out of sight, there were still plenty of craft which ventured inshore to take a look at the proceedings. The French replied with all the cannon and mortars they could bring to bear, but their gunners found it very difficult to judge ranges over water, and the British usually got away unscathed.

Three times a week in summer, the coast trembled to cannon

fire and volleys of massed musketry, when the army went through its evolutions and mock battles were staged by whole divisions at a time. On such occasions the soldiers enjoyed a little relief from the endless round of drilling and inspections that were carried out under the immediate eye of hard taskmasters like Soult and Vandamme.

The years of preparation at Boulogne brought a threefold benefit. Most obviously the army was trained to a high degree of military proficiency:

> 'These troops had a core of veteran soldiers, commanded by officers who had almost all won their spurs on the field of battle. Moreover the entire body was put through endless manoeuvres and marches, drilled to the point of exhaustion, and subjected to the most exact discipline. Thus the soldiers became a force to be reckoned with, especially in the hands of the Emperor.'[8]

Secondly, the common ordeal did much to overcome the memories of France's divisive past:

> 'Generals, officers and soldiers lived in perfect harmony, for in their eyes the devotion they bore towards their sovereign was the same as the one they harboured for their country. Members of aristocratic houses like Caraman, Lameth, Saint-Chamans, Latour-Maubourg, Nicolay and Narbonne were glad to be counted the equal of people like Merlin, Tholozé, Petiet, Montbrun and Mouton.'[9]

All ranks now identified themselves closely, even fanatically with their units, and the newly-discovered sense of regimental pride found a deadly expression in an outbreak of duelling.

Lastly Napoleon consolidated his personal hold over the army. He paid several visits to the encampment, most memorably on 16 August, 1804, when he decorated a number of individuals with the Legion of Honour in the presence of the whole army. This occasion was remembered as probably the most impressive military spectacle of the Napoleonic period.

> 'The combined army came to more than 60,000 men. The Emperor wore one of the uniforms of his Guard, and he sat on a throne

12

surrounded by the colours he had taken from the enemy in Italy and Egypt. At his side were seated the princes, the great dignitaries and the marshals, and the army was drawn up on every side. You can imagine the effect of 60,000 men arrayed in a fairly narrow hollow, not to mention more than 20,000 sightseers who had come from all the neighbouring towns . . . 2,000 musicians and drummers sounded martial airs, and the batteries of cannon beat out the time . . .'[10] 'The sight of the army, the camps and the forts, together with the resounding thunder of the waves and the cannon, and the view of the white cliffs of England, all served to arouse our enthusiasm. The noble scene was lit by the rays of a splendid sun.'[11]

A number of old Republicans had been put out by the proclamation of Napoleon's Imperial dignity on 18 May, 1804, but by the time of the actual coronation on 2 December most of them had succumbed to the general intoxication. In any case the ceremony seemed a little superfluous, because in the eyes of his soldiers 'he had already received the finest consecration possible, that of victory'.[12]

What kind of army was Napoleon building up for the war in 1805? The term *Grande Armée* covered the regular land forces of the French Empire, or in round numbers 446,000 troops, of whom nearly 200,000 were to be committed to Napoleon's campaign in central Europe. About half of the total were veterans of the glorious past. The rest were drawn by conscription from a united population of at least 30,000,000 souls.

The largest single formation was the army corps. This was a self-contained fighting entity comprising a main force of two or more infantry divisions, together with a brigade or division of light cavalry destined in particular for scouting, a couple of companies of heavy corps artillery, and detachments of engineers and other service troops. Napoleon made and re-made the complements according to the needs of the moment, and in 1805 the size varied between the 41,000 troops of Soult's massive IV Corps, and the diminutive VII Corps of Augereau which stood at less than 15,000.

The corps were the foundation of Napoleon's strategy, being at once capable of independent movement, and of combining their action for a common end. The *émigré* gunner Comeau saw Napoleon's host in operation in the combats between Elchingen and Ulm, and he was astonished at the ease with which those huge formations worked together:

'This great army had aroused my surprise and scorn at five in the evening, but by seven the next morning I was lost in admiration. The six component corps acted as one, though each was strong enough to wage a vigorous campaign on its own account. They were led by six marshals, acting under the authority of a superior, a sovereign who alone could inspire unison and harmony in such a mass . . . I found it amazing and novel to see these confused masses of troops give birth as if by magic to the divisions, columns of attack, and imposing concentrations which Ney managed like the experienced soldier he was. There was not the slightest friction or delay, and this army had scarcely assembled at the assigned locations before it launched an energetic and well-calculated offensive . . . this was the first time I had seen how these masses could break through to an objective, hold off part of the enemy force while crushing the rest, and finally turn back on the troops they had kept in check and annihilate them in their turn.'[13]

The corps was the accepted command of one of the marshals, a rank created by Napoleon in 1804. These dignitaries surprise us as much by their youth as by their diverse social origins. Of the marshals present at Austerlitz, Davout, Soult, Lannes, Murat and Bessières were all in their middle thirties, while Bernadotte was one of the old men of the army at forty-one.

Making some rough generalizations, we can say that Davout was probably the most thoroughly professional of these commanders, that Murat was the most dashing and the most stupid, that Lannes had the best eye for a tactical situation, and that Bernadotte was the one who was least trusted by Napoleon. Soult, however, had a special place in Napoleon's esteem, as the tireless disciplinarian of the camp of Boulogne, and the man who was going to direct a crucial attack at Austerlitz. Bigarré flatly declared that 'of all the commanders in Europe, Marshal Soult is the one who is most skilful at moving large masses of troops, and exploiting them to the best advantage on the battlefield.'[14]

The infantry division was made up of one or more brigades, each containing two regiments, and a dozen guns. This produced a total of between 5,600 and 9,000 troops. General de Pelleport describes the creation of the 18th Division, which was put together at Strasbourg from the 26th Light Regiment, the 3rd, 18th and 75th regiments of the Line, and two battalions of sharpshooters:

'These ten battalions comprised about 9,000 combatants. The division had a train of artillery corresponding to its size, and an administration which was responsible for supplying its needs. No particular body of cavalry was assigned to the division, though cavalry was provided from outside according to circumstances. The baggage was reduced to the absolute minimum, so as not to impede the march. Such in brief was the organisation of an infantry division of the *Grande Armée*. After several months of campaigning the division became in every respect a consolidated whole. There were no intrigues, no jealousies, and you could see that the component troops were all animated with the same spirit.'[15]

Thus the habit of working together was instilled into all the formations of Napoleon's army, and it was to give the French an incalculable advantage in the campaign of 1805.

The infantry regiment was composed of three or four battalions. The battalion in its turn was made up of six (originally nine) companies, namely one of grenadiers (carabiniers in the Light regiments), one of *voltigeurs* and four of fusiliers (*chasseurs à pied* in the Light regiments).

These grenadiers were tall and reliable men. The *voltigeurs* were just as good in their own way, but were chosen from smaller and more agile folk who were especially fit for skirmishing.

The regiments of infantry were variously designated as Line or Light. In August, 1805, there were eighty-seven of the former, and twenty-six of the latter. The organization and equipment of the two categories were identical, but the supposition was that the Light regiments would be used in situations where there was a special call for mobility. The full field establishment of a regiment was usually reckoned at 3,400, and of a battalion at 1,100, though in the campaign of 1805 there were many units which could muster little more than one-third of these numbers.

As a further complication, a number of infantry regiments furnished extra élite companies to make up a special combined grenadier division of five regiments. However the main infantry reserve consisted of the foot grenadiers of the newly-proclaimed Imperial Guard. These were for the most part youngish but experienced soldiers, who enjoyed superior relative pay and rank to the rest of the army. An exotic complement of *chasseurs*, mounted grenadiers, *chasseurs à cheval*, dragoons, lancers, Egyptian Mamelukes, *gendarmes d'élite* and detachments of gunners and sappers brought the number of the Guard up to about 12,000, of whom 5,500 were present at Austerlitz.

All categories of infantry were armed with the Charleville Model 1777 musket, a light (16.5 mm) well-made weapon which helped to give the French a tactical edge over the Russians, who carried a variety of clumsy guns.

Most commonly the French infantry went into battle with some of their troops thrown ahead in a loose skirmishing order, and the rest following behind in a mixed formation of lines and columns. The three-rank line was the norm, and the basic tactical 'brick' was the 'division' of two companies. The Line regiments of Soult's Corps at Austerlitz were disposed in column of division, making up four regimental columns, or two lines of battalion in column, depending on the way you looked at them. Soult writes:

> 'The divisional generals were expressly urged to retain the forma-
> tion of two lines of battle and one of light infantry, and to keep
> the battalions in (tactical) divisional column, at platoon intervals,
> so that they could operate with greater speed, while being able at
> any time to form square against cavalry. This arrangement was
> maintained throughout the action, and if some battalions deployed,
> it was only to present a greater extent of front to the enemy.'[16]

The organization of Napoleon's cavalry was relatively simple, comprising the division of two or three regiments, the regiment of four or more squadrons, and the squadron of two companies or troops. The nominal establishment of the regiment stood at upwards of 1,000 mounted men (up to 1,800 in the case of the *chasseurs à cheval*), though in campaign conditions it seems to

have been rare for a regiment to put more than 500 into the field.
The complications come with the subdivision of the types
of cavalry. In August, 1805, Napoleon's horse was made up of
twelve regiments of cuirassiers, two of carabiniers, thirty of
dragoons, twenty-four of *chasseurs à cheval*, and ten of hussars.
The carabiniers and the armoured cuirassiers counted as heavy
cavalry, whose job was to deal massive hammer blows on the
battlefield. The dragoons, or medium cavalry, were a versatile
breed, capable of fighting alongside the heavy cavalry, but also
trained to provide escorts in the rear, to carry out raids and
reconnaissances, and even to operate on foot with their muskets.
The light cavalryman — the *chasseurs à cheval* and the hussars —
could also play a dashing rôle on the battlefield, but their true
qualities were best shown in tasks requiring speed and mobility
away from the main body of the army.

The regiments of cavalry were usually grouped together in
homogeneous brigades of heavy, medium or light cavalry. The
brigades of light cavalry were frequently assigned in penny
packets to the various corps (see p. 13), while a high proportion
of their heavier brothers were concentrated in Marshal Murat's
massive cavalry reserve of 23,500 troopers, who were to play such
a prominent part in the campaign of 1805, covering Napoleon's
sweep into Germany, and being held in a body on the left flank
of the field at Austerlitz.

Generally speaking, the French cavalry was less well-drilled
and well-mounted than the prime regiments of the Russians and
Austrians. France was perpetually short of horses, and Napoleon
gave priority to the transport of his guns. However, these weak-
nesses were more than offset by the *coup d'oeil* and enterprise of
the French colonels and generals, who threw their depleted
regiments with terrible effect against the flanks and rear of the
allied cavalry.

Napoleon began his military career as a gunner, and his name
as a tactician is above all associated with the use he made of his
formidable artillery. This was composed of a standard range of
4-, 8- and 12-pounder cannon, and 6- and 8-inch howitzers. The
new 6-pounder cannon was still a rarity in 1805. In recent years

General Marmont had reorganized the arm in an impressive fashion, and by 'militarizing' the drivers he brought the complement of the corps to no less than 38,000 men. One company of gunners was assigned to every battery of between eight and twelve pieces. There were twenty-two such companies in each of the eight regiments of foot artillery, and six in each of the six regiments of mobile horse artillery.

The batteries were in turn apportioned in such a way as to achieve heavy concentrations of fire. Most of the lighter guns were formed into the divisional reserves, while some horse artillery and the very effective 12-pounders were earmarked for the corps reserves and the army reserve, and therefore stood at the immediate disposal of the higher commanders. As we shall see, it was the timely arrival of six 12-pounders from the IV Corps reserve which turned the course of the battle on the Pratzen heights at Austerlitz.

The other technical arms do not figure very largely in the campaign of 1805. The military engineers found no defended fortresses to besiege, while the pontoon train rarely caught up with the rapid march of the heads of columns of the army.

The medical 'care' was rudimentary in the extreme. Bandages and medicaments were scarce, and even the meticulous Marshal Davout was unable to procure waggons to transport his wounded to the dressing stations. If many of the wounded survived the campaign, it was only because all large-scale movement ended soon after Austerlitz, and because Baron Larrey, the chief of the Grand Field Hospital, carried through a ruthless policy of amputating shattered limbs.

It is difficult to identify anything that could reasonably be called a French supply system in the campaign of 1805. Napoleon left himself with too little time or money to fit the army out with an adequate complement of supplies and transport, and he merely required the columns to provide themselves with four days' rations of bread and four more of biscuit, which were to be issued to the men only when a battle was imminent. From the testimony of Davout we know that the commissariat was unequal to meeting this modest demand, that pay was well in arrears, and that many of the guns had to be left behind on the march.

1. Emperor Alexander

General Kutuzov, nominal commander the allies at Austerlitz.

3. Lieutenant-General Bagration, commander of the allied right at Austerlitz.

4. Russian Imperial Guardsmen. *Left to right*: Preobrazhensky,
Semenovsky and Izmailovsky regiments.

These circumstances would have proved fatal for any army except Napoleon's, which swept through Central Europe with undiminished momentum. Food was available in relative abundance through the agency of the authorities in Württemberg and Bavaria, and in Braunau and again in Vienna and Brünn Napoleon gathered up vast quantities of clothing, ammunition and ordnance which were obligingly abandoned to him by the enemy. In any case, apart from a minimum quantity of essential commodities, Napoleon was not bound by a conventional system of supply. As Levasseur points out:

'The Emperor's energetic way of warfare demanded that his forces should be free of those numerous supply columns which armies used to drag about with them, and which so delayed their movements. He knew that he had to enter the field from September, for by that time of the year every village, every house even, offered him a ready-stocked magazine of victuals and fodder.'[17]

The Revolutionary Wars had already bred up a whole generation of heartless marauders, skilled in the arts of plundering the peasantry, and 'it would be untrue to say that any great number of their comrades disapproved of what they were doing. Their reputation depended solely on their performance on the battlefield, where they invariably showed themselves to be the bravest of men.'[18]

Altogether the *Grande Armée* of 1805 was the finest force which Napoleon ever took into the field. Three years of hard training had overcome the indiscipline and negligence that were the legacy of the Directory, and aroused just sufficient frustration to put the troops in the mood to make short work of whatever Austrians or Russians first presented themselves to their bayonets:

'All the ambitious young men were galvanized by the idea of the coming campaign. Every one of them was dreaming of the prospect of glory and rapid promotion, and they hoped to distinguish themselves in the eyes of their leader. He was the idol of his army, and he had the secret of involving his men with him in the unbelievable activity of his affairs.'[19]

At thirty-six Napoleon was already tending to plumpness, and he wisely affected the noble simplicity of the dark green undress uniform of a colonel of the *chasseurs à cheval* of the Guard, over which he commonly wore his famous grey riding coat. He was still capable of the great physical exertion that was one of the major requirements demanded of an effective commander in those days. Apparently immune to fatigue, he put in a fourteen-hour working day, and travelled by preference on horseback when on campaign. He spent the nights in whatever palace, abbey, farmhouse or shed came to hand, or occasionally in his efficiently-appointed coach.

The vast apparatus of Imperial headquarters was designed to channel information to the person of the Emperor, and to transmit his orders in the most efficient manner. Thus the direction of the *Grande Armée* was centralized to a remarkable degree. In 1805 Napoleon's personal headquarters, the *Maison*, numbered no less than 400 officers and 5,000 men; the heart of the organism resided in the topographical office, where the swarthy Bacler d'Albe kept stores of maps, together with coloured pins and chalks ready for Napoleon to use in their heated planning sessions. Reports, returns and records were the business of the General Headquarters, which was supervised by Marshal Berthier.

Napoleon wrote to Berthier from Paris on 7 September asking him 'to let me know whether you have carried out my instructions, namely to entrust somebody who is acquainted with German to follow the march of the Austrian regiments, and file the details in the compartments of the box you were told to make for that purpose. The name or number of each regiment is to be entered on a playing card, and the cards are to be changed from one compartment to another according to the movements of the regiments.'[20]

However, Napoleon's conception of intelligence embraced not only the numbers and dispositions of the enemy forces, but their morale and efficiency, and the nature of every possible theatre of war. As a further preliminary to the campaign he commissioned Captain Bernard and the generals Bertrand and Savary to go their several ways and sound out the routes through Swabia.

For the first weeks of the campaign additional intelligence

reached Napoleon from the most daring of his spies, Charles Schulmeister. A master of disguise, Schulmeister could alter his appearance in an instant by rearranging his expression and running his fingers through his hair. He passed himself off as a dealer in spirits and tobacco, and he contrived to insinuate himself into the headquarters of the Austrian commander Mack, who treasured him as the best of *his* spies. Among other things, Schulmeister was able to inform the French about the movements of Werneck's corps, and tell them that Kutuzov was determined to avoid battle. Schulmeister's imposture was detected about half-way through the campaign. Even then his legendary luck held true, for his Austrian guards merely escorted him for some distance, then beat him up and let him go.

Napoleon strove for information to the very end, and in the tense days before Austerlitz he sent envoys like Savary to the Russo-Austrian camp to sense the mood of the allied high command. Bearing all this effort in mind, nothing is more surprising in 1805 than the ignorance of all the combatants as to where exactly the enemy armies were. Napoleon's cavalry served him dismally in this respect. On the day after Austerlitz the allies were saved from total annihilation only because Napoleon was misinformed about the direction of their retreat.

We have space to touch only very lightly upon Napoleon's style of warfare. Aiming always at the destruction of the main armed force of the enemy, he concealed his first movements behind screens of cavalry, then used the corps system of miniature armies (see p. 14) to sweep forward and bring his forces together in sudden and decisive concentrations. To the old-fashioned armies the word 'concentration' merely signified heaping together troops on a given spot. Napoleon's massing of strength was of a different order, which derived from a rational articulation of forces over a wide theatre of war. Thus he preserved a wide choice of options until he judged the time was ripe to bring on an action.

Napoleon managed his battles like a campaign in miniature. He usually began the action on a wide front, so as to confuse the enemy and pin them down. Then, when the hostile army was off balance, he liked to throw a *masse de rupture* against a chosen sector of the line.

Contemporaries were misled by what seemed to be the limitless daring of the man. In fact Napoleon was the most hard-working and cautious of commanders, who constantly insured and re-insured himself by creating fortified retreats and alternative lines of communication on campaign, and by husbanding large tactical reserves on the battlefield. He fully subscribed to the eighteenth-century doctrine that you should fight only when you had a very good chance of beating the enemy. If he seemed so much more adventurous than the old generals, it was only because he was so clever at arranging things to his own advantage.

Napoleon reinforced the physical effort of the *Grande Armée* by a psychological war of endless variety. He commonly adopted an imperious tone when dealing with his enemies, in accordance with the Palmerstonian principle of 'the more you ask the more you are likely to get'. In the days before Austerlitz, however, it suited his purpose to appear diffident and anxious, an act which he performed so well that the enemy conceived the very rash project of attacking him.

The famous bulletins of the *Grande Armée* were a tissue of half-truths and downright falsehoods, and the phrase 'to lie like a bulletin' gained some currency as a result. In 1805 they reveal amongst other things a determined attempt to influence opinion in Austria. Thus Napoleon wrote flatteringly about revered Austrian historical figures like the Empress Maria Theresa, and he was careful to depict Austria's allies variously as plundering savages (the Russians) and merchants in human flesh (the British).

In the proclamations that were more directly addressed to his own army, Napoleon took pains to stimulate the pride of his soldiers, while demonstrating a fatherly concern for their welfare. Not the least of his gifts was the ability to create a feeling of cameraderie with the men he happened to meet on campaign, and we know from the memoirs of the period how the reports of such encounters were broadcast and treasured. However, the Emperor possessed an almost infinite repertoire of guises, according to the impression he wished to create. Nothing could be more appalling than the effect when Napoleon chose to direct his anger against some individual or body. The Count de Saint-Chamans overheard him berate the 4th Regiment of the Line, which had lost an eagle standard at Austerlitz. Saint-Chamans was only a spectator, 'yet I must own that my flesh crawled. I broke into a cold sweat, and at times my eyes were coursing with tears. I do not doubt that the regiment would have performed miracles, if it had been led into action at the very next instant.'[21]

CHAPTER 3

THE ARMIES OF OLD EUROPE

I THE AUSTRIAN ARMY

THE Habsburg army destroyed by the French in 1805 was in many ways the peculiar creation of Lieutenant-General Carl Baron Mack von Leiberich. Mack was born on 25 August, 1762, to an undistinguished Protestant family in Franconia. As a youngish officer he was fortunate enough to come under the wing of the all-powerful Field-Marshal Lacy, and he entered the 1790s with a title of nobility and the reputation for being a first-class staff officer. After a spell of service in the Flanders campaigns, Mack earned himself further favourable attention in 1794, when he brought out his *Instructionspuncte für Generals*, a work which breathed the spirit of the offensive.

People began to entertain their first doubts about Mack's judgment when he commanded the Neapolitan army in a disastrous campaign in 1799. He actually fell into the hands of the enemy, but in the following year he slipped away from France in breach of his parole. From that time, he had lived in semi-retirement on his Bohemian estate.

Mack was rescued from obscurity by the cabinet minister Ludwig Cobenzl, who saw him as the one military man who was prepared to put his bellicose schemes into effect. In the middle of April, 1805, Mack composed a glowingly optimistic report on Austria's ability to mobilize for a new war, and on the 22nd of that month he was appointed *Genéralquartiermeister*, or chief of staff. The poor Archduke Charles retained only a vestige of authority as nominal minister of war. After one of Mack's more spectacular tirades Charles complained to Cobenzl, 'This man is perfectly crazy!' The minister merely replied, 'Ah well—he is useful, and that is enough!'[1]

The Austrian army was much less battleworthy than Mack supposed. The monarchy had been almost continuously at war since 1792, and Archduke Ferdinand confided in his diary:

> 'we exist in gloomy apathy. Austria . . . is labouring under a grossly defective state administration. Some of the men in charge of internal affairs are simply not up to the job . . . Our provinces are groaning, and particularly the new acquisitions . . . The finances are in ruins, and we are heavily oppressed by debts.'[2]

The military budget was slashed by more than one half, from 87,371,000 florins in 1801 to 34,402,000 in 1804. Most of the troops were sent home on leave, to save the expense of keeping them with the colours, and the transport trains for the supplies and artillery were disbanded altogether. The majority of the infantry still carried the Maria Theresa musket of 1754.

Although the Habsburg states were vast in extent, the realizable military resources were very small compared with those of France. Conscription extended only to the heartland of the monarchy— the 'Hereditary Lands' of Austria proper and Bohemia and Moravia, with a population of some 13,000,000. About 12,000,000 more dwelled in lands like the Tyrol, Hungary, Transylvania, Austrian Italy or the newly-acquired Galicia, which were privileged, unreliable or otherwise left out of the reckoning. To fill the gaps, Austria still had to resort to the unpredictable means of voluntary recruiting.

Both the Austrian and Russian forces were 'regimental' armies on the eighteenth-century pattern. In other words they had no semi-permanent subdivisions like the brigade, the division or the corps, which provided the French with convenient intermediate stages between the mass of individual regiments and the entity of the army as a whole. For the allies, terms like 'column', 'corps' or 'brigade' signified no more than an *ad hoc* arrangement of regiments or battalions. On the approach to the field of Austerlitz, the

Russian General Langeron was appalled to see that the chiefs were not given the slightest opportunity to get to know their units:

> 'In these five marches the individual general never commanded the same regiments from one day to the next. Night always fell before we reached camp. The orders arrived late, and there was nothing to be done about them in the darkness; it was a time of full moon, but the sky was laden with clouds and the atmosphere was misty, so that no useful light could get through. With the coming of morning every general had to send to the other four columns for the regiments which were supposed to make up his own command. These units sometimes had to march an additional couple of miles to reach him. It was invariably ten or eleven before we could gather ourselves together. Often the columns got in each others' way, or passed through one another—a blunder which would be impardonable in the lowliest and most ignorant staff officer. The forces reached their destination late, and broke up in search of food. The villages were ransacked amid scenes of abysmal disorder.'[3]

Thus the ill-fated General Prebyshevsky was introduced to his column just one day before the crucial battle.

On 14 June, 1805, not long before the outbreak of war, Mack gained the Emperor's permission to reorganize the infantry regiments. Each was now to comprise four battalions of fusiliers and one of grenadiers, made up of four companies apiece. At 800 men to the fusilier battalion and 600 to the grenadier battalion, the regiment possessed a nominal establishment of 3,800 troops. New regulations for the infantry and cavalry were introduced at the same time.

Archduke Charles had no objection to change as such, but he pointed out that by embarking on novelties at a time of tension the army ran the risk of 'having to enter the field when the old order had been overthrown, yet without the time to introduce and consolidate the new way of doing things'.[4]

In the event some of the regiments had to rearrange themselves while they were actually marching to the theatre of war, and nobody had the opportunity to get used to the new organization and regulations.

The Austrian tactics were complicated and rigidly formal, and they emphasized the power of solid formations of 'regular, well-drilled and steady infantry'. In 1804 Archduke Charles visited the exercise camps at Pest, Austerlitz and elsewhere, and he noted that the movements of the regiments were disorderly, laboured and slow. These failings could be attributed to the unfitness of the troops on returning from leave, the presence of many raw recruits, the negligence of some of the officers and not least a dire shortage of ammunition. We come across a characteristic order from Archduke Ferdinand dated 1 October, 1805: 'Since many of the newly-arrived troops have still to be trained in musketry, I approve the issue of six live rounds to be fired by every such man.'[5] This was hardly the way to produce eagle-eyed marksmen.

Probably the most enthusiastic troops of the Austrians were the regiments of Croatian light infantry from the south-eastern borders. Napoleon's spy Schulmeister reported that 'the *Grenzer* battalions are stronger than the Austrian battalions, and their soldiers give a more military and healthy impression'.[6] Unfortunately these troops had also received only a sketchy training, and the Austrians did not exploit the opportunity of using them in the manner of the French *tirailleurs*, skirmishing ahead of the massed formations in line and column.

The Austrian cavalry comprised eight regiments of armoured cuirassiers, six of dragoons, six of the excellent *chevaulégers* (a kind of light dragoon), twelve of hussars and three of lancers. The regiments were organized into eight squadrons of varying complements, according to the type of cavalry, which produced a nominal total of more than 1,400 for the cuirassiers and dragoons and over 1,700 for the rest. Even Mack did not dare to tamper with the organization, which had last been decreed in 1801, but he made his meddlesome presence felt by reducing the line of battle from three ranks to two.

The Austrian artillery was a relic of the eighteenth century. The gunners stood on a totally inadequate establishment of 11,260 men, who were divided into four regiments of sixteen companies apiece. According to a bad old system the gunners had to borrow unwilling labour from the infantry to fill out the gun detachments. Likewise the teams of artillery horses had to be created anew every time hostilities broke out, and as a consequence the Austrians embarked on the campaign of 1805 with only half the full complement.

The tactical organization was an outmoded one. As was the eighteenth-century practice, most of the lighter guns were distributed in penny packets among the infantry battalions as *Linien Artillerie*, and only the remnants were preserved in batteries as *Reserve Artillerie*. Thus the Austrians rarely achieved a concentration of fire, and it was only as a result of an accident that Major Frierenberger's powerful train of artillery reached the field of Austerlitz on a crucial sector (see p. 130).

The range of Austrian ordnance had probably been the finest in Europe, when it was introduced back in 1753. By the time of the campaign of Austerlitz, however, every piece was outmatched by its French equivalent, as we can see from the following table:

Austrian pieces		*French pieces*	
TYPE	CALIBRE IN MM	TYPE	CALIBRE IN MM
3-pounder cannon	75	4-pounder cannon	84
6-pounder cannon	96	8-pounder cannon	106
12-pounder cannon	116–120	12-pounder cannon	121
7-pounder howitzer	150	6-inch howitzer	165

Mack was bewitched by what he imagined to be Napoleon's method of warfare, and he was determined to make the Austrian army follow the French practice of living off the country. He wanted the Emperor to declare that 'those senior supply officers who do not understand it, or who do not want to understand it, will be thrown out and replaced by better ones'.[7]

Mack carried through this 'reform' with an evident lack of intelligent analysis. When the regiments entered Bavaria in September, they were relieved of their remaining supply waggons, and left to search not just for food, but for pack horses, cavalry remounts and clothing. Whereas the French troops had acquired a marked cunning and ruthlessness at this kind of thing over the years, the Austrians merely wandered in an amiable and helpless fashion over the countryside. That was why the Austrian command found it so difficult to concentrate its forces for the combats around Ulm.

Mack never even tackled one of the chief causes of the Austrians lack of mobility. A veteran had complained:

> 'Almost every day our army loses half a march to the French. Their soldiers carry the same load as our men, but what an effort it takes us to get under way! The French officer accompanies his troops on foot, and if necessary he carries his pack himself. In our army, on the other hand, every company has a whole tail of carts solely to transport the officers' baggage. If possible, these gentlemen would like to bring along warm stoves and arm-chairs as well.'[8]

Taking into account the heavy cuts in the ordinary regimental transport trains, the proportion of the officers' baggage in the units actually increased in 1805.

Thanks to the pioneering work of Field-Marshal Lacy in the previous century, staff duties were the one branch of the military art in which the Austrians excelled. This was one of the fields in which they were called upon to help the Russians, who proved to be scarcely capable of moving without the presence of their borrowed Austrian staff officers and topographical guides. The Russians hated to go a-begging in this way, and they did not hesitate to blame their misfortunes upon the Austrian advisers, with their 'impracticable' schemes. Relations between the two parties were not improved by the fact that the Russian calendar ran twelve days behind the western version.

The Russians were also heavily dependent on the Austrians for supplies. To enable Kutuzov's column to take the field, the Austrians delivered more than 400 officers' horses, 6,000 pairs of boots, 50,000 pairs of shoes, a quantity of tents, forty-two field pieces and a quantity of ammunition equivalent to 150 rounds per gun. The consignment of musket ammunition was apparently broken down into loose powder and lead bars, since the Austrian calibre was smaller than the Russian.

The Russian army had also undergone a period of relative disorganization and uncertainty. From 1796 until 1801 the Russian forces had been the obsession of the fanatical Tsar Paul I, who was completely besotted with the image of the Prussia of Frederick the Great. He dressed the soldiers in an attractive imitation of the Prussian military fashions of the Seven Years War, and he allowed free rein to his favourite Alexei Arakcheev, an extreme disciplinarian. Thus 'in almost every respect the Russian army was set back by half a century'.[9]

Paul was forcibly dispatched to the great celestial drill square in 1801. His son and successor, Alexander I, was a man of milder temper, who preferred to manage affairs at one remove. He set up a new Ministry of Land Forces, and established a Military Reform Commission under the presidency of his brother, the Grand Duke Constantine.

The effects of this break of continuity soon displayed themselves in the command of the army. The older type of Russian general was characterized by a disinclination towards book-learning and a love of creature comforts in the field. In 1805 the prime exemplar was the wily Kutuzov, who owed his survival as much to his nose for the atmosphere at court, as to his skill in campaigning against the Turks.

Buxhöwden was another one of this ilk. He was an Estonian German who had advanced himself by marrying an illegitimate daughter of the Tsarina Catherine. In the course of the Austerlitz campaign he established his headquarters in the house of the parish priest of Kutscherau in Moravia. His host described him thus:

'a man of extreme conceit and pride, but also, if I am not mistaken of very little education . . . The French were at some pains to get acquainted with the neighbourhood with the help of maps. Buxhöwden, on the contrary, carried about with him a train of hunting dogs, as well as other creatures which I shall not specify out of fear of offending the ears of decent people. The whole took up eleven coaches and as many carts, and the entire space of the vicarage, so that the quantity of riding horses for himself, his generals and servants, and the vast quantity of his sentries, came to no less than 96 animals, with 139 attendant personnel.'[10]

The best of the Russian command was probably to be found among the middle-ranking generals like Dokhturov, Miloradovich and the *émigré* Langeron. The finest of the breed was undoubtedly the forty-three-year-old Prince Bagration, a fiery and utterly reliable leader, whose Georgian ancestry was proclaimed by his dark eyes which gleamed from an otherwise hard and immobile face.

Alexander's inclinations drew him more to the company of aggressive and arrogant aides-de-camp like Wintzingerode, Lieven, Volkonsky and Dolgoruky. He displayed a particular partiality for anyone who could spin elaborate plans, full of the exact minutiæ of clever manœuvres, like the ones which so entranced him in the mock campaign at Peterhof in 1804. The older generals were justifiably aggrieved that rank and seniority were being so blatantly circumvented. In former days, wrote Buxhöwden, the junior officers used to harbour the deepest respect for their seniors:

> 'But at the present time authority has declined to such an extent that everyone from ensign to general treats one another with the same familiarity. A sentiment of indifference and disrespect has insinuated itself in the relations between subordinate and commander, and we have forgotten the awe which is indispensable among military men.'[11]

Thanks to a century of Romanov despotism, Alexander had an almost unlimited supply of manpower at his disposal. A total of 43,785,000 people lay under tsarist rule at the time of his accession, and the greater part of the men were 'liable' to a term of military conscription lasting twenty-five years. Call-up went ahead almost unchecked during the years of peace, and it was intensified as the new war approached. In 1805 a levy of four out of every 500 young 'liable' men produced an influx of no less than 110,000 recruits. Altogether the Russian land forces approached 300,000 regular troops, together with 100,000 cossacks, and recruits and other elements which brought the grand total to more than 500,000.

The Imperial Guard in its glittering array was the formation closest to the person of the Tsar. In 1805 it comprised a number of small but select regiments of horse, one battalion of *jaeger*, and three regiments of infantry—namely the Preobrazhensky (3,000), the Semenovsky (2,264) and the Izmailovsky (2,264). The men of the Guard were chosen for their stature and bearing, and the officers were reckoned to be probably the finest of the army.

The officers of the line cavalry also enjoyed a high reputation. On the other hand most of the officers of line infantry were 'disqualified by the neglect of education, and the absence of those accomplishments which should distinguish officers as well as the sash and the gorget . . . The want of regimental officers is more felt in this army than in any other in Europe.'[12]

The physical endurance of the Russian soldier was legendary, and foreign observers were struck by the obedience, frankness and self-respect he usually showed in front of his superiors. The adherents of the Arakcheev school of thought treated their men badly, but the majority of officers regarded their charges as reasonable beings. Even Paul's Tactical Rules of 1797 pointed out that 'the soldier will do more for an officer who treats him well, and wins his trust, than one he simply fears'.[13]

When the Russian soldier did run out of control, he displayed a mindless barbarity that was the terror of all in the surrounding theatre of war. Yet even here his instinct was to gather in large bands under chosen leaders, with the ultimate ambition of returning to his beloved homeland. 'The Russian, nurtured from earliest infancy to consider Russia as the supreme nation of the world, always regards himself as an important component of the irresistible mass.'[14] On a field of battle, desperately wounded Russian soldiers used to drag themselves eastwards just to die a little nearer home.

The green-clad Russian infantry was formed of seventy-seven regiments and two battalions of musketeers, thirteen regiments of élite grenadiers, and twenty regiments of *jaeger* (light infantry). The Military Reform Commission placed all the regiments on a uniform establishment of 2,256 for the regiments of musketeers and grenadiers, and 1,385 for the *jaeger*. Of the three battalions of the musketeer regiment, one was designated a grenadier battalion. Thus, taking into account the Guard and the grenadier regiments proper, we end up with three categories of élite troops. All the regiments were now called after their recruiting areas, which helped to foster a sense of cohesion among the men.

In the year of Austerlitz the tactics of the Russian infantry were still supposed to conform with two rule books which dated from the previous reign—the *Military Code Concerning the Field Service of Infantry* (1796) and the *Tactical Rules for Military Evolutions* (1797). There was great stress upon military carriage and appearance, as we might have expected from something produced by Paul I. The soldier marched with his stomach in and chest out, with the right arm motionless by the side, and the left arm fully extended to hold the musket upright. There was no bending of the knee, and at every step the foot slammed the ground toes first. The tactical rate of march was established at seventy-five paces to the minute, though a 'quick' march of 120 paces was added in 1803.

The code of 1796 sought to impose linear tactics after the Prussian style, and the whole emphasis was now put on the firepower of the three-rank platoon. The platoon column was made the basis of every movement, but for purposes of combat against infantry the regiment was supposed to deploy into line and open a rolling fire, with the four platoons of each company discharging volleys in succession. An attack in échelons, or staggered formation of platoons, was advocated in certain circumstances, and the *Tactical Rules* of 1797 recommended the use of squares to withstand cavalry.

In the campaign of 1805 the generals interpreted these codes with a certain latitude. All the senior officers had campaigned at one time or another under the revered leadership of Generalissimo A. V. Suvorov (1729–1800), who was a firm advocate of the bayonet, and it must be more than a coincidence that so many of the commanders claimed that they had delivered attacks with cold steel. Kutusov actually stipulated on 18 October that 'it will often be necessary to form battalion columns, whether to pass through a line, or to deliver an attack more effectively in difficult terrain'. He added:

'We shall often have to exploit the peculiar prowess of the Russians in bayonet attacks. The following points are therefore to be noted and obeyed with the greatest exactitude:

1. The cry of *Hurrah!* is the one that brings us victory. Nobody is to dare to utter it until the command is given by the brigade commander, at the very lowest.
2. During the attack with the bayonet the front of the formation is to be held as straight as possible, so that nobody will run ahead.
3. Upon the command "Halt! Dress!" the battalions will come to an instant stop.'[15]

While combat in dispersed order was supposed to be the special province of the *jaeger*, Kutuzov was willing to extend the tactic to all the infantry, if they had to pass through thick woods or other obstacles.

The burden of the evidence leads us to suppose that the infantry codes of 1796 and 1797 were in fact of less importance than the whim of the commander on the spot. In any case, actual combat rarely corresponded with the tactical ideal. Platoon fire very soon degenerated into a general blazing-away. As for the attack with the bayonet, one side or another almost invariably ran away before bayonets were crossed.

In 1803 Alexander carried through a general lightening of the regular cavalry, which reduced the number of cuirassier regiments to six, and increased the dragoon regiments to twenty-two. The hussars stayed the same at eight regiments, though one of this number had been converted in the previous year to a regiment of uhlans (lancers). The regiments of cuirassiers and dragoons were on a field establishment of five two-company squadrons (rather over 1,000 per regiment) and the hussar regiments on an establishment of ten squadrons (about 1,900 per regiment).

With local modifications, the tactics of the cavalry were determined by Paul's *Code of Field Cavalry Service* (1796).

Paul decreed that 'the company or squadron is always arranged in two ranks, for experience shows that the third rank is useless—it impedes nearly all the movements, and when anybody falls it proves dangerous to rider and horse'.[16] In the attack against opposing cavalry, the cuirassiers and dragoons gradually built up

. Men of the Russian Shabrichesky Grenadier Regiment.

6. Austrian infantry.

their speed from the slow gallop to the 'course', and then to the full gallop. At eighty or one hundred paces from the foe the commander ordered a fanfare to be sounded and shouted *Marsch! Marsch!* whereupon the troopers were supposed to raise their swords and fall on the enemy. The cavalry acted with more circumspection against infantry, manœuvring by small detachments so as to avoid musket fire.

The hussars were useful people to have on the battlefield, in view of the large establishment of their regiments, but they were more specifically trained to guard the flanks of the army, to furnish chains of outposts, and to undertake raids and reconnaissances. They were not expected to engage in a serious way unless they were fully confident of success, 'for less disgrace attaches to an hussar officer who retreats, than to one who gets embroiled with the enemy in unfavourable circumstances'.[17]

The swarms of irregular horse were rather more expendable. The Military Reform Commission pointed out that 'when the need arises, the (regular) cavalry can always be reinforced in a short time by cossacks and other irregular forces, which do not put us to the useless expense of maintaining them in peace'.[18]

In time of war up to 100,000 cossacks could be put into the field. By far the largest contribution was made by the Don Cossacks, with smaller forces hailing from the Bug, the Black Sea coast, the Urals, Siberia and the south-eastern steppes. The weapon *par excellence* of the cossack was the lance. It was 'the toy of his infancy, and the constant exercise of his youth; so that he can wield it, although from fourteen to eighteen feet in length, with the address and freedom that the best swordsman in Europe would use his weapon'.[19] On the battlefield the cossacks liked to put in wheeling attacks against the flanks of enemy units. In general, however, the cossacks were happiest when they were roaming free over the countryside, plundering with equal disregard enemy stragglers and innocent peasants.

Russian armies have always marched to battle with a formidable array of interesting ordnance. By the time of Austerlitz, General Arakcheev had already been at work for more than three years on reforming the artillery. He began to introduce light gun carriages and caissons on the Gribeauval pattern, and he reduced the variety of pieces to a range of 6- and 12-pounder cannon (in light and medium versions), and 3-, 10- and 20-pounder unicorns (long barrelled howitzers). The artillery was assigned according to weight to 'light' or 'heavy' companies of twelve pieces each. Between four and seven such companies went to form every mixed artillery regiment of more than 2,000 officers and men.

However, the Russian artillery was still not quite a match for the French. Not only were the numerous unicorns badly outranged by Napoleon's long guns, but too many of the weapons were scattered piecemeal among the regiments. Thus at Austerlitz it was only on their left that the Russians achieved a heavy concentration of ordnance. It was some compensation that the Military Reform Commission had assigned a permanent establishment of draught horses to every company. The animals were speedy enough over firm ground or snow, though they were unequal to pulling the Russian guns through the wet clay of Austerlitz.

The story of the artillery is representative of the Russian army as a whole, where the value of men and material was nullified by a lack of ensemble. The commissariat system was sketchy and improvised, which made for a high rate of 'strategic consumption' even when everything else was going well. There was little unity of command in the field, and above all there were no native staff-trained officers capable of giving direction and cohesion to the effort of the individual arms.

The stupidity of the people in charge of the Russian army seemed to one of the Austrians to be

'beyond anything you could believe possible. They are absolutely useless for anything that has to do with manoeuvre, and in this respect an ordinary French soldier is worth more than all the officers of the Russian army put together. The Russians are brave enough in combat, but their gallantry goes for nothing because they do not know how to direct it or use it to strike home. They charge with the bayonet . . . but they are so clumsy that they never manage to catch anyone.'[20]

CHAPTER 4

THE RUIN OF THE AUSTRIANS AT ULM

THE Austrian preparations for war exhibit a curious transition from half-measures and prevarication to an almost panic-stricken scramble. The initial hesitations sprang from the fear of provoking Napoleon into taking the offensive before the allies had come together. Mack, therefore, set to work at a leisurely pace, gradually recalling the men from leave, and buying up horses to move the guns and supplies. We shall shortly see that the timetable failed to keep pace with the speed of events, which forced the Austrians to push their disorganized troops piecemeal into the conflict.

As for the detailed plan of operations, the Austrians believed that they ought to put their weight into northern Italy, where they were fairly certain that Napoleon intended to deliver the main offensive, as in 1796 and 1800. Here, at least, Archduke Charles exercised a decisive influence. He had submitted a memorandum on the subject on 3 March, 1804, pointing out that the French would have to trail all the way across Swabia and Bavaria in order to get at Austria by way of northern Europe. In northern Italy, on the other hand, the rival forces would be face to face—the French in firm possession of their Italian annexations and puppet states, and the Austrians penned up in the corner of north-eastern Italy behind the Adige. A defeat on this theatre promised to be disastrous, for there would be nothing to stop the French from pushing through the unfortified Alpine provinces of Carinthia and

Styria to Vienna. 'The Adige must therefore be considered the first and most preferable theatre of war.'[1] Thus it was decided that Charles in person was to take the offensive in Italy in 1805 with no less than 90,000 troops, with Archduke John covering the right flank in the Tyrol with 22,000 more.

The plan for the Danube valley was thrashed out on 29 August, 1805. The issue hinged on the 70,000 or so troops that were allocated to the northern theatre, and how their operations were to be supported by the 50,000-strong Russian army of General Kutuzov, who was going to march all the way from Poland.

The most sensible ideas were put forward by Archduke Ferdinand d'Este, the nominal commander of the Danube army. He was a twenty-four-year-old Italian princeling, closely related to the House of Habsburg. His appointment (unlike most of the kind) reflected the fact that he was an intelligent and energetic soldier, well acquainted with the theatre of war. Ferdinand sensibly asked the conference to consider the danger of up to 150,000 Frenchmen irrupting into the neutral territory of Bavaria before the allies had assembled, and he urged that the Austrians must act cautiously, advancing their first 30,000 or 40,000 troops only as far as the Bavarian capital of Munich. The Emperor Francis was at first inclined to agree, but Mack argued forcefully that the Austrians should sweep forward without waiting for the Russians, so as to win the resources and army of Bavaria, and cover the passes leading to the Tyrol. Like the cabinet minister Colloredo, he assumed that everything could be calculated in such a way that the French could not possibly intervene before the Russians arrived: 'All anxiety on this head is unfounded.'[2]

With the advantage of hindsight, the British ambassador Sir Arthur Paget was able to perceive two radical faults in the Austrian grand strategy.

The 'first and principal fault which has been committed was to have taken the field (in Bavaria) with too small a force'. By July, wrote Paget, there were clear indications that Napoleon would make his move in Germany, and in any case it ought to have been obvious that the troops from the camp of Boulogne would be campaigning on the northern theatre rather than in Italy. Paget found the explanation in the tensions in the Austrian high command. Mack was aware that Charles was hostile towards him, and he probably did not want to sharpen the antagonism by asking for troops to be withdrawn from the Archduke's command in Italy. 'To this false and misplaced delicacy therefore are in great measure owing the present misfortunes.'

Secondly there was the overhasty advance into Bavaria, which assumed more speedy co-operation from the Russians than was actually forthcoming, 'from whence . . . the Austrians voluntarily and with their eyes open chose to commence hostilities single-handed against the French'.[3]

The advance elements of the Austrian army on the Danube set out from the camp at Wels on 5 September, 1805, and over the next few days they poured across the Inn into the unresisting territory of Bavaria. The Elector Maximilian of Bavaria persuaded Mack that he was willing to join the coalition. He meanwhile shuffled his little army out of the way to the valley of the upper Main, where it ultimately declared for the French.

Mack's enthusiasm was fired by a premature report that the French had already crossed the Rhine at Strasbourg, and he drove his dusty and exhausted troops westwards across Bavaria to the river Iller, which was one of the south-bank tributaries of the Danube. Archduke Ferdinand in person reached Munich on 19 September, clad in his new authority of a full general of cavalry. He attempted to stem the crazy onrush, but he was overborne by Mack, his nominal subordinate. By the end of September about 43,000 Austrians were strung along the 138 miles between the Inn and the Iller at Ulm. The improvised supply arrangements (see p. 28) collapsed completely, and the cavalry and artillery were dragging on behind. Thus the troops went hungry in a fertile land, and the army was breaking up before it had so much as encountered the enemy.

Mack was unperturbed. He accepted the confusion and disorder as part of the way things were done in this modern age. Strategically he was sure that his arrangements were comprehensive and balanced: he was confident of checking the French frontally in the passes of the Black Forest, or in the worst case along the line of the Iller, where he was throwing up fortifications at Kempten, Memmingen and Ulm; away to the south Lieutenant-General

39

Jellačić had more than 11,000 troops on the approaches to the Vorarlberg and the Tyrol; to the north, Mack was certain that his right flank would be covered by the inviolably neutral Prussian territory of Ansbach, which jutted into south-western Germany. As an additional safeguard, Lieutenant-General Kienmayer was posted on his right rear at Neuburg on the Danube, where he would gather the reinforcements coming from the interior of the monarchy, and establish contact with the Russian army of General Kutuzov, whose arrival was confidently expected on the theatre by 20 October.

Napoleon, however, was not the man to allow the allies to assemble their forces in peace. Having renounced the invasion of England (see p. 10) he unrolled a vast seven- by ten-foot map of Europe over the charts of the Channel, and began to ponder where to direct his forces. As he accumulated information about the allied movements, so he determined with ever greater precision how he was going to crush his enemies somewhere north of the Alps.

In broad outline Napoleon intended to feed his cavalry reserve across the upper Rhine and into the Black Forest, thereby amusing the Austrians on the southern sector, and meanwhile bring his forces from Boulogne, Holland and Hanover on a vast wheel into Swabia so as to irrupt against the Austrians on their right flank and rear. Altogether 194,000 French troops were committed to the decisive operations in Germany. At the time of the passage of the Rhine they comprised:

Corps	Commander	Inf. divs.	Cav. divs.	Bns.	Sqs.	Numbers
I	Bernadotte	2	1	18	16	17,737
II	Marmont	3	1	25	16	20,758
III	Davout	3	1	28	12	27,452
IV	Soult	4	1	40	12	41,358
V	Lannes	2	1	18	16	17,788
VI	Ney	3	1	25	12	24,409
VII	Augereau	2		16	4	14,850
Cav.	Murat		6		120	23,415
Guard	Bessières			12	8	6,278
						194,045

30,000 men remained on the Channel coast, and Marshal Masséna with 50,000 troops was to tackle the Austrians in northern Italy, with General Gouvion Saint-Cyr guarding his rear with 18,600 in central Italy.

The move from Boulogne began on 27 August. The French were fundamentally land animals, and 'no departure was more brisk or more cheerful. The gunners abandoned the coastal batteries as easily as if they had been marching out of barracks, without anyone to relieve them. The soldiers greeted the cruising English warship with cries of *Vive l'Empereur!* and there was not a single one of them who would not sooner have marched into the depths of Siberia rather than invade England.'[4]

Marching respectively from Hanover and Holland, the corps of Bernadotte and Marmont seem to have had the shortest and easiest route to the theatre of operations. Conditions were harder in the centre, where the corps of Davout, Soult, Ney, Lannes and the Guard marched from north-eastern Frence to reach the middle Rhine on the 110-mile stretch between Mainz and Strasbourg. A grenadier of the Guard recalls that 'we marched by platoons day and night, without being given an hour of sleep. We clung together in ranks to prevent ourselves from falling. Whenever a grenadier did collapse nothing could awaken him, even if he fell into a ditch and was belaboured with the flat of a sword. The music sounded and the drums beat the charge, but nothing could master our desire to sleep.'[5] The corps of Marshal Augereau came up behind, traversing the entire width of France from Brittany to the upper Rhine.

Soult's finely-disciplined IV Corps reached the Rhine at Speyer in twenty-nine days, with scarcely a man lost on the way. On the southern sector the Guard and other troops entered Strasbourg in varying degrees of exhaustion from 20 September (some arriving unconscious on carts), and they bivouacked along the streets, among the horses, artillery and vehicles. Lannes got across the Rhine at Strasbourg on 25 September. He was closely followed by Murat and the cavalry reserve, which fanned out towards the Black Forest according to the plan of operations.

Napoleon deliberately lingered at Boulogue until 3 September, knowing that his whereabouts would be followed by many interested observers. He had hoped to be in Germany on the 17th, but he found himself annoyingly delayed at Paris by the need to sort out problems caused by a severe shortfall in taxation. The Emperor finally left Saint-Cloud on 24 September, and he reached Strasbourg two days later:

> 'His arrival was announced by salvoes of artillery and peals of bells. The majestic procession was led by a guard of honour, splendid in its youth and costumes. The progress was greeted by repeated acclamations, and the people of Alsace flooded along the route like a torrent. In the evening, by the light of the illuminations, the spire of the cathedral was a fiery column suspended in the air.'[6]

In the last days of September the *Grande Armée* set over the Rhine by ferry and bridge. The mood of aggressive confidence was caught by the division of Vandamme, which was due to cross the water at Speyer:

> 'On the evening before the passage, all the commanders of the division were invited to dine with the general. In the course of the meal he asked the master of the house for coffee. This individual rudely replied that he had no coffee to spare for Frenchmen. General Vandamme was not the man to suffer impertinence, and he instantly replied with a blow. The coffee was not slow to appear.'[7]

On 29 September, when the eastward march was well under way, Napoleon proclaimed to the *Grande Armée*: 'Soldiers, the War of the Third Coalition has begun. The Austrian army has crossed the Inn, violating international law. It has attacked our ally and chased him from his territory.'[8]

Without too much poetic exaggeration, the descent of the *Grande Armée* from the Rhine to the Danube may be compared with a tornado, twisting its way out of the sky, and curling downwards to work chaos and destruction on the earth. The start line along the Rhine measured 160 miles. Sixty miles into Germany the direction of march began to veer to the south-east, with the inner columns (Murat, Ney and Lannes) pivoting around Stuttgart, and

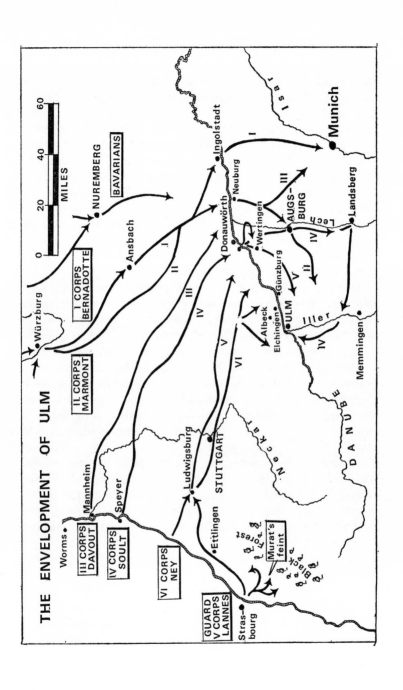

THE ENVELOPMENT OF ULM

MILES
0   20   40   60

BAVARIANS

NUREMBERG

I CORPS BERNADOTTE

Würzburg

II CORPS MARMONT

Worms

Mannheim

III CORPS DAVOUT

Speyer

IV CORPS SOULT

VI CORPS NEY

GUARD V CORPS LANNES

Stras-bourg

Murat's feint

BLACK FOREST

Ettingen

STUTTGART

Ludwigsburg

Neckar

Ansbach

Donauwörth

Neuburg

Ingolstadt

Wertingen

AUGS-BURG

Landsberg

Munich

Isar

Lech

Günzburg

ULM

Elchingen

Albeck

Iller

Memmingen

DANUBE

the outer columns (Bernadotte and Marmont) sweeping past Würzburg. As the wheeling movement became more pronounced, so the columns drew closer together, creating a funnel which came to rest on the seventy-mile reach of the Danube between Ulm and Ingolstadt.

As the commander of the corps which now had the furthest to go, Bernadotte barged straight through the Prussian territory of Ansbach on 3 October. By way of retaliation the Prussians now allowed the Russians the right of passage through Silesia, but otherwise they chose to swallow the insult. More diplomatically inclined than Bernadotte, Napoleon was meanwhile busy establishing good relations with his south German clients. He called on the Duke of Baden at Ettlingen on 1 October, and on the next day he proceeded to Ludwigsburg, where he obtained a promise of aid from the Duke of Württemberg.

Counting the Bavarian forces which were gathered on the way, Napoleon crossed Germany with a spearhead of something like 75,000 infantry, 30,000 cavalry and 400 guns. The time taken was less than two weeks, and the distance amounted to 120 miles for the innermost corps, and to more than 200 for the outer elements.

Like most famous marches of history, this movement showed a well-calculated urgency rather than breathless haste. The intervals between the sub-columns were carefully apportioned, so that all the troops could take their share of the potatoes in the fields, or whatever food was brought out by the friendly villagers. The regiments set off early each morning, and with any contrivance they were able to complete their assigned march by noon, leaving the troops free for the rest of the day to go foraging. While Davout wrung his hands at the indiscipline of some of his troops, the morale of the *Grande Armée* remained remarkably intact, even when the splendid weather of the previous few weeks gave way to a prolonged spell of icy rain.

Altogether the progress of the host was at once curious and impressive. The Emperor

'rode a series of horses which he borrowed from the Duke of Württemberg. The generals took their mounts from the post offices, while many other officers were still on foot. There was no body of troops in any recognizable order. Instead a compact mob of infantry flooded across the roads, the fields, the meadows and marshes. It was impossible to make out battalions or divisions, for all the forces were thrown together. Behind this mass you could see whole clouds of stragglers.'[9]

By 4 October, when his advanced troops were within striking distance of the Danube, Napoleon was reasonably sure that the Austrians were heaping up their forces in the area between the Lech and the Iller. His counter-strategy was simple and appropriate. He aimed above all to transfer a powerful force to the south bank of the Danube and seize the line of the River Lech up to Landsberg, thereby interposing a powerful barrier behind the Austrians. This task was entrusted to the cavalry of Murat and the two corps of Lannes and Soult, which were to force the Danube at Donauwörth.

The rest of the army was to lend support in various ways. Up the Danube to the west Ney with his VI Corps would contain the Austrian left-bank bridgehead at Ulm, and make ready to establish lodgments of their own on the south bank. Well downstream from Donauwörth, Davout and Bernadotte were to set across the Danube at Neuburg and Ingolstadt respectively, and liberate central Bavaria in the direction of Munich, thereby setting up a deep 'zone of security' to the east.

On the night of 6/7 October the leading elements of Soult's corps reached the Danube. The retreating Austrians had damaged the bridge at Donauwörth by fire, but a couple of miles upstream the French discovered a bridge intact at Münster, and Vandamme's division crossed without resistance. Napoleon in person reached the Danube on the 7th, and he was at last able to satisfy his desire to see the fabled river—at first sight disappointingly small, as it slid past the painted houses of the quaint little town of Donauwörth.

The main striking force was well across the Danube by 8 October, and on that day Murat's dragoons destroyed an isolated force of 6,000 Austrians under Lieutenant-General Auffenberg, who was standing passively at Wertingen. Napoleon learnt from the demoralized prisoners that the bulk of the Austrian army was still deployed to the west of the Lech and that he was therefore firmly established between the Austrians and their homeland. 'From this moment commenced that species of warfare by which the French rendered themselves so remarkable and so formidable in former campaigns.'[10]

It is curious to reflect that though we are already advanced in our narrative, the action at Wertingen represents the first real passage of arms between the allies and the *Grande Armée*. There cannot have been many wars where such a great deal had been decided before the rival forces had so much as come to grips.

Meanwhile at Ulm all sorts of unpleasant truths were coming to light concerning Lieutenant-General Mack. It took a letter from Emperor Francis to persuade Archduke Ferdinand of the truth of a fact which he had earlier refused to credit—that Mack, although nominally a subordinate, had been made the *de facto* commander of the Austrian army, responsible directly to Vienna. The titular command had been invested with the high-born archduke just to keep it out of the hands of the Russians, who would have refused to serve under a nobody like Mack.

More unsettling still was Mack's fanaticism on the subject of Ulm, which he described as 'the queen of the Danube and the Iller, the bulwark of the Tyrol, and the key to half Germany'.[11] He had about 70,000 troops at his disposal, counting the outlying detachments of Jellačić and Kienmayer (see p. 40). The French he estimated at 80,000 at the very most, and considered that they would be fighting against all the disadvantages of geography. Ferdinand had correctly divined Napoleon's strategy as early as 1 October, but Mack's only response was to intensify the concentration around Ulm, which he planned to use as an offensive base. On this and most other points Mack was beyond reason.

> 'From the very commencement of the campaign there existed a degree of jealousy and misunderstanding among the general officers in that army which led to . . . fatal consequences . . . By degrees it arrived at such a pitch, that no communication took place between the commanders in chief (Mack and Ferdinand), *but in writing*. No general officer would attend General Mack unless accompanied by another general officer to bear witness of what passed.'[12]

We have in Mack the first of the nineteenth-century neo-Napoleonic commanders, the kind of man who believed that generalship consisted of grand cure-all strategies, ceaseless undirected activity, and dashing off orders peppered with urgent phrases. He took up scheme after scheme, carried it half way to execution, then abandoned it altogether. Thus the news of the action at Wertingen was enough to persuade Mack to call off an intended march eastwards to force a passage over the Lech. He then hatched a plan to cross to the north bank of the Danube below Ulm, and act against the French communications. He was neatly anticipated by Ney, who forced the passage of the Danube at Günzburg on 9 October and established a bridgehead on the south bank. The Austrians streamed back through the rain to Ulm, exhausted by all the marching and countermarching, and disheartened by their repeated defeats at the hands of the French.

On 11 October Bernadotte reported that the approaching Russian army was still 180 miles away. At the same time Napoleon finally appreciated that the main concentration of the Austrians was at Ulm, and he saw that he now had the chance to eliminate the whitecoats before they could be joined by their Russian friends. He wrote to Soult that he anticipated a battle that would be ten times more famous than the victory of Marengo and he spurred on his soldiers by reminding them of the perfidy of Albion: 'But for the army in front of you, you would be in London today. We would have avenged six centuries of outrage, and restored the liberty of the seas.'[13] It is surprising how often he returned to this theme in the campaign of 1805.

The general trend of the French army was now to the west. Already in firm possession of the city of Augsburg (which was being transformed into a new base of operations), Soult's IV Corps was describing a wide circuit to the south of Ulm. Landsberg was occupied on 9 October, and Soult pushed on for four days through a vast tract of dripping pine forest to reach the area of Memmingen, which was thirty miles south of Ulm. The corps of Bernadotte secured Munich, with Davout guarding the north-west approaches. Otherwise the whole of the *Grande Armée* was now directed straight at Ulm.

The discipline of the French began to suffer under the ordeal of prosecuting forced marches in the appalling weather. As he rode towards Ulm, Napoleon began to pass scenes of considerable disorder:

> 'The roads had completely broken up. They were littered with bogged-down carts from Alsace, with their despairing drivers, and their foundered teams of horses, which were dying from hunger and exhaustion. On every side our soldiers were running about in disarray. Some were in search of food. Others were shooting hares, which were to be seen in abundance on these plains.'[14]

It was lucky that Mack remained unaware of the fate that Napoleon was planning for him. On 11 October the Austrians gained a solitary success when 25,000 of their troops probed along the north Danube bank from Ulm and pushed back the ragged division of General Dupont, whom Ney had left in an isolated position at Albeck. The Austrians returned tamely to Ulm, without exploiting the opportunity to break out to the north. Worse still Mack read from some captured documents that the French had established a new line of communication further to the east, and he reached the false conclusion that Napoleon had left Ulm on one side and was marching directly against the Russians.

Building on this supposed information, Mack set in train a grand scheme to bring all his forces to the north bank of the Danube and strike downriver, cutting the French communications as he went and ultimately joining the Russians. On the morning of 13 October, however, Mack learnt that powerful French forces were on the right bank of the Danube, sweeping towards the southern approaches to Ulm. Mack chose to link this information with unfounded rumours to the effect that the British had landed at Boulogne, and that a counter-revolution had broken out in France. From all of this he drew the extraordinary deduction that the French were making their circuit around the south of Ulm with the sole purpose of marching home.

In the subsequent muddle of orders and counterorders, Mack held back 14,000 troops at Ulm, but was unable to recall the two 'corps' of Werneck and Riesch, which had already set out to fulfil the orginal plan for the attack down the north bank. Once more

Ney frustrated the Austrian schemes by executing a timely passage of the Danube, on this occasion from south to north. On 14 October, while Riesch was struggling through a zone of sodden clay, the marshal came at him by way of a hastily-repaired bridge at Elchingen. The French stormed the village at bayonet-point, then pressed on to beat the last Austrian resistance in the lightly-wooded country behind.

Werneck with his 9,000 men and the heavy guns made off to the north, hotly pursued by Murat, and lost contact with the main body of the army. Riesch fell back to Ulm, which was now closely beset on all sides. At this juncture Lieutenant-General Abele implored Mack to gather his forces together and break out towards the Tyrol. Mack seemed to go crazy: 'he screamed and shouted, behaving in a way that was truly insane. In his fury he advanced on me in a threatening manner, and I feared that I was about to suffer violence at his hands. I backed towards the door with the intention of making my escape, but he came after me and got in the way . . .'[15]

Ferdinand had no intention of exposing his archducal person to the danger of being captured at Ulm, and he plotted with Lieutenant-General Schwarzenberg to break out with 6,000 cavalry along the Geislingen road to the north. He hoped in the fullness of time to gather up Werneck, Kienmayer and the other scattered Austrian forces, and perhaps do something of interest in Bohemia or on the lower Danube. Ferdinand and his chosen band thundered out of Ulm at midnight on 14/15 October. Inevitably the French cavalry was close on their heels.

On the 15th Napoleon brought the bulk of his force to the north bank of the Danube over the Elchingen bridge, and in the afternoon Ney stormed and took the redoubts on the Michelsberg immediately outside the city walls. The Austrians fell back to Ulm under torrential rain.

> 'The appearance of the city was appalling. Many thousands of men made their quarters on the open streets, where they cooked and slept. Carts and teams were standing everywhere. More than thirty dead horses were littered about, for the gates were shut and they could not be carried away. The whole city was a latrine, permeated with a pestilential stench.'[16]

Napoleon now opened a bombardment of the defenceless place, and sent the staff officer Ségur to demand Mack's surrender. Ségur travelled through a furious and wet night and reached Mack's inn at three on the morning of the 17th. He found the general to be 'tall, aged and pale. His expression indicated a lively imagination, and his features betrayed a state of anxiety which he was trying to conceal.'[17]

Ségur pressed for the surrender of the Austrian troops as prisoners of war. Mack was in no position to refuse the demand, but he hoped that he could still bargain for a little time—time for Ferdinand and the others to make good their escape, and time if possible for Kutuzov and the Russians to arrive in the offing. At about noon on the same day Mack agreed to deliver his army into captivity on 25 October, if no relief arrived before that date.

Even this feeble resolution was soon eroded. The morale of the Austrian army was beyond all repair, for the soldiers resented the fact that their officers were to be freed on parole, and as if in sympathy the appalling weather of the previous two weeks outdid itself in a storm on the night of the 18th, whereupon the Danube burst its banks and carried away all the corpses which had not yet been buried. 'They were floating on the river like the débris of some wrecked vessel.'[18] Finally on the 19th Napoleon summoned Mack to the monastery of Elchingen, and informed him that Werneck had been overhauled by Murat two days earlier and forced to surrender.

Without further reference to his generals Mack agreed to deliver Ulm on the following day, on condition that Ney's corps remained immobile in the area until the 25th, and that Marshal Berthier signed a formal declaration to the effect that the Russian army was still impossibly far away.

At two in the afternoon of 20 October the rains stopped as if by magic, and the Austrian army began to wind out of Ulm into brilliant sunshine. To the scandal of the more professionally-minded of the French, the enemy troops cast aside their cartridge pouches and muskets with 'a joy that was almost indecent'.[19] The Emperor was standing with his back to a large fire (his coat tails were actually smouldering), and he spoke sympathetically to the party of seventeen Austrian generals who were around him. A

French officer asked one of the whitecoats to have the kindness to point out the Austrian commander. The dignitary replied 'the man standing before you is the unfortunate Mack in person'.[20]

The force which Mack surrendered at Ulm consisted of fifty-one battalions, eighteen-and-a-quarter squadrons and sixty guns with their detachments, or in round figures between 23,000 and 24,500 men. This was not the end of the disaster. The old and methodical General Jellačić was overtaken by the recently-arrived VII Corps of Marshal Augereau, and forced to surrender with most of his surviving men at Dornbirn on 14 November. Ferdinand had meanwhile fled by way of Ansbach to Bohemia, dropping stragglers all the way. The Archduke reached Eger on 23 October with just 1,892 men and 1,794 horses. Of the army which had marched into Bavaria, only Kienmayer's detachment escaped the *débâcle*. Altogether the Austrian loss must have amounted to nearly 60,000 troops.

The coalition reeled under the blow. The ailing Prime Minister Pitt felt that even the great naval victory of Trafalgar (21 October) could not restore the balance, and the hopes of drawing Prussia into the alliance immediately faded, despite a visit which Tsar Alexander was paying to Berlin.

These were long-term considerations. Far more urgent was the fate of the band of Russian troops under General Kutuzov, which was marching along the Danube to link up with an Austrian army which had ceased to exist.

CHAPTER 5

KUTUZOV BREAKS FREE

IN fulfilment of the grand scheme of operations (see p. 6), Kutuzov set out on 25 August from Radziwilow, on the borders of Russia and Austrian Galicia. At the start he had 46,405 troops under his command, divided into six columns which marched off at strictly-controlled intervals. A few days into Galicia Kutuzov received an order to send the sixth column back to observe the frontier with Turkey. He informed Emperor Francis of what had happened, breezily remarking that where the Russian army was concerned, courage was more important than numbers. Francis could scarcely be expected to agree, and he wrote urgently to Alexander asking him to have the troops sent back again. Thus the Russian column made another about turn, and trekked wearily back towards the Danube some way behind the parent body under Kutuzov.

On 22 September Kutuzov reached Teschen, at the boundary of the Austrian provinces of Galicia and Moravia. Here he received a plea from the Austrians to hasten his march at all costs, for news had come that Napoleon had left the camp of Boulogne and was advancing on Germany. Kutuzov did his best to comply, but pointed out that 'our soldiers have already endured much fatigue, and they are suffering badly'.[1] Soldiers and officers alike were now ordered to leave their baggage behind, and horses were drawn from the supply train so that at least the vital ammunition carts could keep up with the regiments. Fortunately the Austrians made available 2,233 two-horse carts, and Kutuzov decreed that 'the first part of each column must always go ahead on the vehicles, so that it can complete the first half of the march before the rearward part of the column, which comes up on foot'.[2] The soldiers had to enjoy what rest they could on the jolting vehicles, because Kutuzov allowed just one day of rest after every four on the road. It proved quite impossible to transport the guns at the same rate as the infantry: the horses were already overworked, and 'it would do the service no good to see this important element of the army so exhausted on the way, that it did not have the wherewithal to act when it reached its destination'.[3] Even the regiments of dragoons were forced to travel on foot.

The further march of the Russians took them by way of Brünn to the Danube valley at Krems. Already on 1 October Kutuzov had to represent to the Austrians that 'the shoes of most of the troops have broken down in the prevailing wet weather. They have had to march barefoot, and their feet have suffered so badly on the sharp stones of the highways that the men are incapable of service'.[4] Thousands of sick and stragglers were being left behind, and Kutuzov now had to allow the army to rest after every three days of the punishing march.

For a few days Kutuzov left the army and betook himself first to Vienna, where he was accorded a triumphal reception on 7 October, and received the congratulations of Francis on the speed and order of his march. He then travelled briskly up the Danube and arrived on the 9th at the fortress of Braunau, which commanded the middle reaches of the Austro-Bavarian border along the Inn. Three days later the first of the Russian troops appeared on the scene, and over the next two weeks the regiments trailed in one after another. By the 26th Kutuzov had collected some 27,000 exhausted Russians along the Inn, together with the 18,000 survivors of Kienmayer's corps, and a wandering detachment of three battalions of Croats and the Austrian Hessen–Homburg Hussars.

The Austrian contingent came under the local command of Lieutenant-General Max Merveldt, who was anxious that Kutuzov should attempt to save the situation around Ulm. Kutuzov refused to commit himself until he gathered his forces and knew more about what was happening in Bavaria. He had received a letter from Ulm dated the 8th, in which Ferdinand explained that the Austrians had 70,000 troops in a good position, and that he looked forward to common operations with the Russians. Unfortunately the Archduke failed to specify exactly what the Austrian army was going to do. Kutuzov remained immobile, and Merveldt wrote to Vienna that although the Muscovite was willing enough, 'he seems unacquainted with the art of war, and especially with operations against the French—a very different proposition from campaigning against the Turks. He leaves time and distance completely out of account, and is most unwilling to risk his troops. All of this will make it difficult to persuade him to advance.'⁵

Disturbing rumours began to percolate to Braunau. They differed in detail, but all agreed that the Austrians had undergone some kind of reverse at Ulm. Finally on 23 October 'an elderly gentleman came to Kutuzov, having important tidings to communicate to him. Could Kutuzov have possibly expected that it was General Mack himself, bearing news of the complete annihilation of the army under his command?'⁶

Napoleon was already taking active steps for the next bound. He gathered ammunition, shoes and other necessities at Augsburg, and as a matter of political necessity he travelled to Munich on 24 October to receive the welcome due to him as the liberator of Bavaria.

Napoleon set himself two strategic aims. The first was to isolate the Danubian theatre of war from all immediate possibility of disturbance from the armies of the Archdukes John and Charles (see p. 38). He accordingly detached a number of formations to sweep the Alpine flank: Augereau with the VII Corps followed on Jellačić's heels into the Vorarlberg (see p. 51); Ney with his VI Corps and the Bavarians was to seize Salzburg and the Tyrolean passes; lastly Marmont and the II Corps were to take the long route to the Styrian-Hungarian borders, and post themselves directly in Archduke Charles' path from Italy.

The second and the more important objective was to destroy Kutuzov and the remnants of Mack's command somewhere on the south bank of the Danube, and seize Vienna before the allies fed more forces into the theatre, or the Prussians made up their minds to enter the war. In fact 'this preoccupation, the fear that the Russians might escape to the north, was the one which dominated Napoleon's thinking throughout the war. No danger was greater for him than the almost inexhaustible resources of the northern powers—of Russia and Prussia. The whole of his campaign in Moravia, and the battle of Austerlitz itself, were conceived in this persuasion.'[7]

Kutuzov was just as determined to preserve himself from the fate being planned for him. He saw the salvation of Vienna as secondary to the necessity of keeping his army intact until he could join the new Russian columns that would soon be arriving on the theatre (see p. 6). On 29 October he sat in council at Wels with Francis and a collection of Austrian generals. They agreed on a compromise strategy, by which Kutuzov would put up a series of obstinate delaying actions behind the south-bank tributaries of the Danube, and finally withdraw into the bridgehead fortifications at Mautern on the Danube just over forty miles upstream from Vienna. A permanent bridge stretched to the north bank opposite at Krems, so that Kutuzov could guard the main road to Vienna and still have a path of escape. The Archdukes John and Charles were now ordered to make in all haste to the Danube from the Alps and Italy. Kutuzov was already recognized as the *de facto* commander of the allies in this theatre, and towards the middle of November he was invested with the formal authority as well.

On 25 October the *Grande Armée* struck east and south-east across Bavaria and inaugurated the second phase of the campaign of 1805. Four days later, just when a clash seemed imminent, Kutuzov ordered a general withdrawal for about sixty miles from the Inn to the line of the River Enns, which was shorter and more defensible. So as to keep a sting in his tail he entrusted his rearguard to the formidable Prince Bagration, and supported him with a powerful detached reserve under Miloradovich, hovering at a distance of half a march between the main army and the rearguard proper. The French found that the Russians were stripping the countryside, and burning the bridges 'in a way we had never experienced before'.[8]

The snow was falling heavily when Napoleon rode into the

abandoned fortress of Braunau on 30 October. The allies had left behind a useful quantity of supplies, and Napoleon transformed the place into the depôt to support the advance of the *Grande Armée* into Austria. As yet the French had failed to make contact with the retreating enemy, though 'we could have followed their track easily enough by the stragglers and sick they left behind'.[9]

The first small clash was staged on 31 October, near the Traun stream at Lambach, where four Austrian battalions were overhauled by the French. They were rescued by Bagration with two battalions of his *jaeger*.

After a two-day halt on the Traun, the allies fell back to the protection of the Enns. Bagration was covering the retreat as usual, and he fulfilled his task so conscientiously that on 4 November he reached the bridge over the Enns only minutes ahead of Murat and the pursuing French. While the enemy raged on the west bank, the Pavlograd Hussars burnt the bridge under a hail of canister, using incendiary materials which had been laid beforehand. This gallant detachment was commanded by Colonel Count Joseph Cornelievich O'Rourke (1772–1849), whose family hailed from County Leitrim. He was at the beginning of a brilliant career, and 'he attracted general attention during this campaign, when he was almost continuously in charge of the rearmost forces. You might say that he bore the weight of the enemy on his shoulders.'[10] Tolstoy used the episode as the basis for a famous passage in *War and Peace*.

Kutuzov did not imagine that he could hold the line of the Enns for very long, but the allies were bounced from the river even more quickly than he had anticipated. Murat lunged against the middle Enns at Steyr, and with seeming cowardice General Merveldt and the main body of the Austrians promptly made off to the southeast. Just four battalions of Austrian infantry and four regiments of their horse remained with the Russians. Only after the war did it transpire that Merveldt was not to blame for the *débâcle*: 'He had received orders and counterorders by the score. That which directed him to remain with General Kutuzov arrived too late; he had *according to orders* (from Vienna) commenced his march towards Styria, and could no longer re-effect his junction with the Russians.'[11]

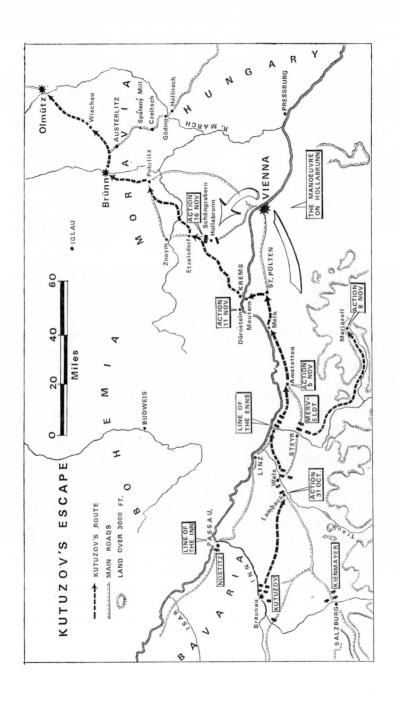

KUTUZOV'S ESCAPE

KUTUZOV'S ROUTE
MAIN ROADS
LAND OVER 3000 FT.

Miles
0   20   40   60

Olmütz

Wischau

AUSTERLITZ

Spáleny Mill

Göding Hollitsch

Czeitsch

PRESSBURG

R. MARCH

H U N G A R Y

Brünn

Pohrlitz

ACTION
16 NOV

Schöngrabern
Hollabrunn

VIENNA

THE MANOEUVRE
ON HOLLABRUNN

M O R A V I A

Znaym

Etzelsdorf

ACTION
11 NOV

KREMS

Dürnstein

Mautern

ST. PÖLTEN

Melk

ACTION
8 NOV

Mariazell

B O H E M I A

IGLAU

BUDWEIS

LINE OF
THE ENNS

Amstetten

ACTION
5 NOV

MERV-
ELDT

STEYR

LINZ

Wels

ACTION
31 OCT

Lambach

Traun

LINE OF
THE INN

PASSAU

NOSTITZ

KUTUZOV

Braunau

B A V A R I A

I N N

I S A R

SALZBURG

KIENMAYER

The wretched Merveldt fell into the path of the two corps of Davout and Marmont, which were sweeping through the outcrops of the Alps. The Austrians were already in a desperate state, 'and the grenadiers harnessed themselves to the guns, and dragged them along while the blood was pouring from their feet'.[12]

On 6 November Davout was hounding the Austrians through the Styrian gorges when he overtook a large convoy of arms, tentage and clothing:

> 'We found that the most useful articles were their sky-blue Hungarian pants, their half-boots, their linen underclothes and their greatcoats. Our *voltigeurs* took the opportunity to arm themselves with sabres. The convoy also contained the complete equipment of an uhlan regiment, together with all the instruments and music folios for the band, and the chaplain's sacred vessels and ornaments. We did not bother to gather these assorted valuables, but tipped all the carts into the gorge so as not to impede the progress of our guns.'[13]

Two days later the greater part of the Austrians were destroyed on the snow-covered fields at Mariazell, leaving Merveldt with a pathetic 2,000 men to reach safety in Hungary.

With the collapse of his left centre at Steyer, Kutuzov was left with no *point d'appui* short of the bridgehead fortifications which the Austrians were supposed to be building more than seventy miles down the Danube at Mautern. The road pushed through almost continuous pine forest, with the inky black Danube coursing just to the left, and the hills rising to 1200 or more feet immediately to the south. There were few clearings where the Russians could have drawn up their forces to halt their pursuers, and in any case Napoleon seldom allowed them the respite. The French troops hastened down the road under storms of rain and snow, plundering the peasants as they went and fighting over the spoils.

On the afternoon of 5 November Murat was pounding through the forest of Amstetten at the head of two brigades of light cavalry. The ground and trees were thickly covered with snow, and one of the party drew his attention to the beauties of the scene:

'the silvery frost softened the strident colours of the dead oak leaves and the sombre green of the pines. Shapes and hues lost their definition under this icy robe, and they appeared more subtle still in the mist, making a delightful picture. Thousands of icicles caught the light and . . . hung from the trees like glittering chandeliers.'[14]

The reverie was dispelled when Murat emerged from the wood and found himself face to face with lines of enemy infantry stretching across one of the rare clearings. For once the allies had contrived to make a stand.

Murat and his staff did an about turn and shot back along the road, followed by a confused mass of French and allied cavalry. The one person who kept his head was the young artillery lieutenant Levasseur, who had been bringing up a pair of 8-pounders. Levasseur manhandled his first piece around, loaded it with a monstrous charge of roundshot and canister, and while the hussars were fighting four paces away,

'Gunner Collot reached out with a lighted match to touch off the piece. At the cry of "Watch out!" our hussars gave way to right and left into the woods, making a little human embrasure in front of the muzzle. A Russian colonel, covered in gold braid and lace, thundered down on my gunner to sever his arm. The shot departed, the barrel broke off at the trunnions, and the colonel collapsed on top . . .'[15] 'the shock caused a mass of snow to fall from the trees onto our heads. As if by magic the squadrons disappeared in a cloud of smoke, and a dense hail of snow, shot and large icicles, some of which descended from more than one hundred feet and clattered on the helmets of the fleeing cavalry.'[16]

After a considerable pause, both sides began to feed heavy forces into the combat. The French sent forward Oudinot's grenadier division to sweep the woods and the open ground beyond, while Miloradovich came back to support Bagration, and advanced the grenadiers of the Smolensk and Apsheron regiments to make a counter-attack with the bayonet.

The combat ended in darkness with both sides claiming the advantage. What was at least certain was that the sharp clash at Amstetten had 'redounded to the honour of the Russian army'.[17]

The French claimed to have killed or captured 2,000 Russians, 'but not a single man surrendered willingly; after they had been wounded, disarmed and thrown to the ground they still put up a fight, and even returned to the attack. At the close of the combat the only way we could assemble a few hundred prisoners was to prod them with our bayonets, like a herd of indisciplined animals, and belabour them with our musket butts.'[18]

The display of obstinacy at Amstetten encouraged Napoleon in the belief that the whole Russian army was going to fight somewhere behind the crag of Melk, with its spectacular Baroque monastery. While he was still girding his loins for the coming 'Battle of St Pölten', he learnt on 9 November that Kutuzov had transferred his entire army from Mautern to the north bank of the Danube at Krems, and burnt the wooden bridge behind him.

Vienna had certainly encouraged the Russians to hold firm on the south bank at Mautern, but Kutuzov had discovered that the much-vaunted bridgehead fortifications had scarcely been begun, and that a French force (the VIII Corps) had set across the Danube at Linz and was working down the north bank to threaten his communications. 'Moreover there were frightful deficiencies in supply, which caused an outbreak of plunder and indiscipline among our forces . . . Most of the regiments were composed of low-grade troops, and we learnt to call our vagabonds by the name of "marauders"—this was the first of our borrowings from the French.'[19] Twenty whole squadrons had escaped across the bridge without authorization, and officers were slipping away from their regiments on the pretence of ill-health.

All the same Kutuzov's escape represented the first major strategic reverse that Napoleon had suffered since he crossed the Rhine. In fact things seem to have slipped from his control for a couple of vital days. He hung about at Linz until late on 9 November, so as to receive a visit from the Elector of Bavaria, and he failed to make clear to Murat that his first priority must be the destruction of the Russians. Murat was not at all concerned at losing contact with Kutuzov, and on the 10th he rushed off in the direction of Vienna, dragging with him not only his own cavalry reserve but the corps of Lannes and Soult as well.

The only force within reach of the Russians was the VIII Corps —a grandiose title for the scratch formation which had been gathered under General Mortier, and dispatched across the Danube by the newly-repaired bridge at Linz. Mortier hurried along the river bank with the single division of Gazan, well ahead of the other two component divisions of his corps, and on 10 November he halted at Dürnstein, which was just over three miles upstream from the Russian concentration at Krems. His liaison with the south bank was virtually non-existent, for the French had been able to gather only fourteen boats on the Danube instead of their intended flotilla of 300.

For once Kutuzov was very exactly informed as to the location and strength of the enemy. His own force had just been increased to more than 40,000 by the belated arrival of the sixth Russian column from the Turkish frontier (see p. 52), and together with the Austrian staff officer Lieutenant-General Schmidt he now hatched a scheme to destroy Mortier at Dürnstein and rid the north bank of the French.

Miloradovich was to engage Mortier frontally, along the river bank, with one regiment and three battalions of infantry, and three squadrons of hussars. General Dokhturov was meanwhile to take to the hills with a powerful column, dropping off General Strik with one regiment and three battalions of infantry to attack the French in the flank, and ultimately descending with most of the remainder to the Danube behind Mortier, so encompassing his destruction.

The Russian movement got under way during the night of 10/11 November. All unsuspecting, the 5,500 Frenchmen settled down beside the Danube. 'Snow covered the ground, and the cold was biting. We maintained our bivouac fires by feeding them with the props which supported the vines.'[20]

In the morning the 4th Light found itself heavily engaged with the troops of Miloradovich as they wound out of the riverside village of Unter-Loiben. 'The Russians were superior in number but they were encumbered by the size of their greatcoats. Their slow movements gave us a great advantage, and we owed our initial success to the clumsiness of the enemy and our own speed in the attack.'[21] The French counter-attacks continued to gain

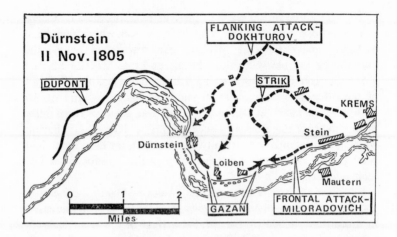

Dürnstein
II Nov. 1805

FLANKING ATTACK-
DOKHTUROV

DUPONT

STRIK

KREMS

Dürnstein

Stein

Loiben

Mautern

0   1   2

Miles

GAZAN

FRONTAL ATTACK-
MILORADOVICH

ground, even after Strik appeared on the flank, and the battle extended into the afternoon.

At five Mortier was congratulating himself on a satisfactory outcome when Dokhturov materialized in his rear at Dürnstein with eleven battalions. Dokhturov had taken much longer over his mountain trek than the plan had anticipated, and he had been forced to leave his artillery by the way. Dokhturov was now in turn attacked in the rear by Dupont with the second of Mortier's divisions, which had hastened along the north Danube bank to the noise of the gunfire.

Thus Gazan's division and Dokhturov's command both found themselves sandwiched between hostile forces. As darkness fell the combat became if possible still more ferocious, and 'on several occasions Mortier in person was forced to kick the more determined of the Russians or chop them down with his sword. He was taller than anyone else, and he became a favourite target in the darkness.'[22]

The battered French broke contact on the 12th and crossed by boat to the south bank. The Russians had lost about 2,000 men, but the French suffered at least as badly, and the division of Gazan was so severely mauled (with up to 1,700 prisoners and casualties) that it took no active part in the rest of the war. Russian commentators have always accorded the action an important place, claiming that this was 'the first time in his military career that Napoleon had been dealt a serious blow in the eyes of all Europe'.[23]

When Kutuzov had every right to feel secure, an extraordinary mischance again placed him in the most immediate peril. Frustrated at Mautern, and humiliated by the reverse at Dürnstein, Napoleon devised a completely new plan to trap the Russians before they could join their allies. While the two corps of Bernadotte and Mortier ferried themselves across the Danube at Melk, the effective advance guard of the *Grande Armée* (Murat's cavalry, Lanne's V Corps and Oudinot's grenadier division) would somehow get across the river downstream at Vienna and race ahead to the area of Hollabrunn, so getting between Kutuzov and the allied reinforcements.

The most unlikely aspect of this famous *manœuvre sur Hollabrunn* concerned the capture of the Tabor Bridge at Vienna, which was the lowest permanent crossing of the Danube barrier. The 'bridge' was in fact a series of rickety wooden structures and connecting causeways, which carried the main road across the thickly-wooded islands and myriad channels immediately north of the city. The last span stretched for no less than 550 yards from the large Wolsau island to the north bank at Spitz. The Austrians declared Vienna an open town, but they had a 'reserve corps' of seventeen battalions and thirty squadrons waiting close by on the north bank under the command of Lieutenant-General Prince Auersperg, who had been revived for the occasion after a dozen years' retirement from active service. A battery commanded the northern exit of the bridge, and the timbers were strewn with straw, firewood and charges of gunpowder ready for immediate ignition. The Austrians were oddly reluctant to destroy their bridges before absolutely necessary, as they showed at Lodi and Arcola in 1796, but the arrangements at Vienna seemed foolproof.

The French first reached Vienna on 12 November. At eleven the next morning General-Adjutant Bertrand and three other officers presented themselves at the first span of the bridge and told the man in charge, the hussar Colonel Geringer, that hostilities had been brought to an end by an armistice. That was a barefaced lie. The puzzled Geringer hastened back to consult his superiors, trailing a mass of French generals, officers and grenadiers behind him.

At the north end of the bridge Captain Johann Bulgarich of the Székler infantry was appalled to see the powerful body of French troops swing into sight around the last bend of the causeway on the Wolfsau. He called to the battery '*Kanoniers! Feuer! die Franzosen kommen!*' The gunners sprang to their pieces, but Lannes, Belliard and several other impressive-looking Frenchmen got among them and persuaded them that they were now all good friends. Meanwhile the French grenadiers sidled forward as inconspicuously as they could, and the gunners and sappers began to cut the fuzes and throw the combustible materials into the river. It dawned on at least one of the Austrians that something was amiss, but 'Marshal Lannes and General Belliard sought to reassure him. They said it was such a cold day that our soldiers were marking time and moving about, just to keep warm.'[24]

Some time in the afternoon Auersperg rode up from the camp of the reserve corps. He found the muzzles of his own battery pointing inland straight at him, and he could see that the bridge was crowded with French. He pressed over the bridge and met Marshal Murat on the second span. Murat brazenly informed him that he would allow the Austrians to withdraw, in virtue of the supposed truce, but he insisted that he must hold the battery. Auersperg rode away, and sent messengers by three different routes to warn Kutuzov that the French were across the Danube.

The episode of the Danube bridge was doubly disastrous. It exposed Kutuzov to destruction, and together with the loss of Vienna it interposed a barrier between the forces gathering in the north and the Archdukes Charles and John in the Alps. The Emperor Francis was 'all the more hurt since this stupid and unpardonable blunder has destroyed the whole trust of my allies at a single stroke'.[25]

The failure of Auersperg to deny the bridge denotes a failure of the will and intellect, if not downright imbecility. The French themselves were taken aback. Fantin des Odoards said it was only natural for a Gascon like Murat to have mystified an Austrian, 'but it seems too much to swallow when a man of such high rank engages his word of honour to prop up a falsehood'.[26] Interestingly enough, once the lead had been given, the allies with all their high titles and long pedigrees were going to prove more adept at fraud than the disreputable French.

The Austrian capital was a valuable prize in its own right. The citizens had been apprehensive for the safety of their persons and property, though very little concerned about the outcome of the war. They detested the savage Russians, and they resented the furtive way in which Francis had departed from the scene. Also the evacuation of governmental property had been carried out with a notable lack of dignity and good sense. Much attention was given to the removal of the archives, 'those even of the Chancery of Bohemia which no Frenchman or foreigner that ever existed would give himself the trouble to read a line of'.[27] On the other hand, no attempt was made to transport the thousands of muskets or the hundreds of guns from the arsenals, or to empty the vast magazines of clothing nearby at Stockerau. Napoleon was presented with all the supplies he needed to continue the campaign unchecked.

The remaining fears of the Viennese were banished by their first encounter with the French. On 13 November Napoleon and his army staged their ceremonial entry:

> 'The sun rose. The Emperor's train was magnificent, what with the embroidery and lace of the coats, the plumes, the fine horses, and the parade uniforms of the *chasseurs*, and the grenadiers and cavalry of the Guard ... the Emperor alone was dressed in severe simplicity ... '[28] 'The shops were open and the markets fully stocked, and the people crowded at the windows and along the streets as if General Mack was making a ceremonial entry to the city.'[29]

Napoleon installed his Imperial person amid the jewel-like parlours and gilded and chandeliered halls of the Schönbrunn. The town palace, the Hofburg, was occupied by General Clarke, who ruled Vienna with the dedicated assistance of the civic guard.

Kutuzov explains that the bloodless capture of the bridge of Vienna 'completely altered my plan. I had intended to defend the passage of the Danube and await our reinforcements in peace. Now I had to hasten my march through Hollabrunn so as to evade combat with the vastly superior forces of the enemy.'[30] His little army had set out from Krems late on 13 November, and on the 14th he received a letter from Francis which made his precarious position only too clear. The route north-eastwards to safety carried Kutuzov past the front of the French, who were debouching from Vienna hardly thirty miles away, and the Russians pressed over the dreadful roads, abandoning stragglers and provisions on the way. This perilous movement was masked by Bagration, who on 15 November took up a position at Schöngrabern with a force variously estimated at between 6,000 and 9,500 men.

The corps of Bernadotte and Mortier were disappointingly slow in getting across the Danube at Melk, due to the high winds and the shortage of boats, but Murat raced over the plain north of Vienna with his cavalry and grenadiers, and on the 15th he approached Schöngrabern shortly after Bagration had settled in his position.

Murat bluffed the Austrian General Nostitz into pulling the Hessen-Homburg Hussars out of their advance post at Holla-brunn, then halted in front of Schöngrabern in the belief that he was facing the main Russian army. He sent word to the Russian commander, proposing that they too should reach an accord, now that the French and Austrians were at peace. Bagration was not taken in by the lie, but he conveyed the message to Kutuzov. Their forces would probably have been destroyed 'if the Russians, with their peculiarly Byzantine cunning, had not contrived to repay the deceitful French in their own coin'.[31]

Kutuzov agreed to discuss terms, and sent the silver-tongued general-adjutants Wintzingerode and Dolgoruky to do what they could to gain time. The French consented to advance no further into Moravia, providing the Russians left Austrian territory by the way they had come. Four hours' notice was to be given of any renewal of hostilities. The deal was supposed to be ratified by Napoleon and Kutuzov, but, as Kutuzov explained to Alexander, he 'delayed the answer more than twenty-four hours, having not the slightest intention of accepting the terms. The army meanwhile continued to retreat and thus gained two marches on the French.'[32]

Bagration passed the morning of 16 November in a state of

Austrian cuirassiers.

8. Lieutenant-General Miloradovich, joint commander of the allied fourth column.

9. General-Adjutant Winzingerode.

10. Grand Duke Constantine, Commander of the Russian Imperial Guard.

11. Lieutenant-General Langeron, commander of the allied second column

justifiable anxiety. 'With my small numbers I remained in the face of a superior enemy, alone and without support, and awaiting the attack at any minute.'[33] Napoleon had meanwhile received the armistice agreement at the Schönbrunn. He at once detected the imposture, and at eight in the morning he penned a scorching note. The Emperor's *billet doux* reached its destination at noon, and at about the same time Murat became aware that the Russian force was smaller than he had supposed. He immediately notified Bagration that he intended to resume the fight, but the stipulated elapse of four hours left him with only a few minutes to get his battle under way before darkness fell. When the combat finally started, a Russian battery of sixteen pieces set the village of Schöngrabern ablaze and imposed a further delay.

The French slowly felt their way towards the main Russian position on a crest 650 yards to the north. Legrand's division worked its way out to the right, while Oudinot's grenadier division and Sébastiani's light cavalry made for the left. However, Bagration was a past master at defending ground in depth. Amid bitter and confused night fighting he withdrew a short distance to a layback position at Grund, then retreated towards the main army by way of Guntersdorf. The fighting retreat was covered by Major-General Selekhov with a battalion of musketeers and a battalion of the 6th *Jaeger*, which twice broke through the encircling French. The little battle ended towards eleven on that freezing night. Hundreds of dead and wounded were being burnt in the flaming villages, spreading 'a frightful stench of roasting flesh for several miles around. It made your stomach heave.'[34]

Fighting against a superior enemy the Russians had lost 2,402 men, of whom 711 were missing, and 737 more were wounded troops who were abandoned to the French. The guns too were left on the field, for the carriages were smashed by artillery fire, and all the horses were killed or maimed. The enemy suffered heavy but unspecified losses. Colonel Pouget was one of the few who passed the night in reasonable comfort: 'The carabiniers of the first battalion prepared me a suitable bivouac—they dragged together a number of Russian corpses, face to the ground, and spread a layer of hay on top.'[35]

Napoleon had set out on the evening of the 16th to join Murat, and while he was travelling through Vienna he could see the northern horizon glowing with the flames of the villages around Schöngrabern. A little later he received some details of his naval defeat at Trafalgar, and he was in an atrocious temper when he reached Znaym next morning to settle accounts with Murat.

Thanks to Bagration's stand at Schöngrabern, Kutuzov's army had passed the dangerous road junctions at Etzelsdorf and Pohrlitz unmolested and was now well into the Austrian province of Moravia. On the 18th Bagration and his rearguard rejoined the main body. Kutuzov came out to meet him. He embraced the wooden-faced Oriental, declaring 'I shall not ask after your losses. You are alive, and that's enough for me.'[36]

On the day before, the Austrian general Prince Liechtenstein brought Kutuzov an ill-assorted corps of Austrians, composed of the remnants of Kienmayer's force and various troops which had been organized too late to reach the war in Bavaria. This accession brought Kutuzov's army up to 45,000 troops, and allies were now on the way to fulfilling 'the principle we have adopted, that of uniting all available forces'.[37]

Falling back deeper into Moravia, Kutuzov reached the capital at Brünn on 18 November, then pressed on to meet the Russian army of General Buxhöwden (see p. 6), who had been diverted from the borders with Prussia to help out Kutuzov and the Austrians. Kutuzov encountered the 14,000 men of Buxhöwden's first column at Wischau on 19 November. One of Kutuzov's officers noted that

'the forces coming from Russia were completely fresh and in splendid order. Our army, on the contrary, had been ruined by perpetual hardship, and broken down by the lack of supplies and the foul weather of late autumn. The troops' uniforms had been destroyed by the conditions in the bivouacs, and their footwear had almost ceased to exist. Even our commanders were arrayed in ill-assorted, almost comic attire.'[38]

The second of Buxhöwden's columns reached the army at Prossnitz on the 21st, and the third and last arrived on the 22nd. The combined Russo-Austrian forces now numbered a mighty 80,000 men.

CHAPTER 6

DUEL OF WITS IN MORAVIA

For the first time in the war the strategic advantage lay firmly with the allies. While the *Grande Armée* appeared to have run itself into the ground, more than 600 miles away from its homeland, all the Russo-Austrian host needed to do was to keep itself in being somewhere in eastern Moravia and wait for the further reinforcements that were sure to flow in from almost every point of the compass. The Russian Imperial Guard arrived in the camp at Olmütz on 24 November in a strength of between 8,500 and 11,000 troops. They had come all the way from St Petersburg, but 'they were a magnificent force, composed of enormous men, who appeared by no means exhausted by such a long march'.[1] They were immediately called upon to grace a magnificent parade in the presence of the Emperors Alexander and Francis.

Yet more reinforcements were on their way from Poland under the command of General Essen, and were expected shortly. Archduke Ferdinand in Bohemia was gathering nearly 10,000 Austrian troops, and was making ready to push eastwards into Moravia. Most significantly of all, Archduke Charles had extricated his powerful army (see p. 38) from Italy in brilliant style, and was hastening to reach the northern theatre. He had given Marshal Masséna a severe mauling at Caldiero on 29–30 October, then fought a series of delaying actions along the river lines of the Venetian plain before disappearing into the Julian Alps. Archduke John now joined him at Marburg with the little army from the

Tyrol. The French held Vienna, on the most direct route to the north, but the Archdukes intended to effect a crossing of the Danube downstream in Hungary.

Napoleon meanwhile behaved with notable circumspection. At his command the Marshals Murat, Soult and Bernadotte urged their weary men to their feet and forced them a last few miles into Moravia. Napoleon arrived outside the fortress city of Brünn on 20 November, and was delighted to discover that it had been abandoned by the allies. In accordance with ancient custom a procession of clergy and municipal notables came out in all their finery to present the keys of the gates to the conqueror. They had to pick their way across sodden fields, and endured an hour of mockery from the French soldiers before they could discover Napoleon. The party was 'out of breath and so spattered with mud that the violet stockings of the bishop and the black stockings of the magistrates were reduced to the same colour'.[2]

Brünn proved to be another 'Braunau' or 'Vienna', stuffed with artillery, ammunition and provisions. Some of the units were lucky enough to be quartered in this fine city, and one of the grenadier captains discovered that it was 'peopled with extremely pretty women, who were got up in the most tasteful and tempting way'.[3] Outside the city, however, the regiments were scattered in squalid bivouacs, half-starved and shivering in the damp cold. Houses were pulled down bodily for the sake of their timbers, and furniture, picture frames and musical instruments were all consigned to the fires.

> 'Our camp presented a dismal sight in the first light of the morning, whenever we shifted our bivouacs. Thousands of scattered fires were still smoking, and around them were littered hunks of beef and pork — the remains of the meal of the evening before — together with battered mattresses, sofas and tables. Peasants picked their way among this wreckage in search of whatever might belong to them.'[4]

These poor people gave the warmest of welcomes to the French, whom they regarded as their liberators from the Russians,

> 'and yet the euphonious name Moravie became the object of a sinister play on words. Many of us believed that the country

signified for them *mort à vie* ('death to life'). Put in these terms the pun must seem childish enough, but at certain times in war, just as in certain periods of our life, a simple pun may correspond to a state of mind . . . In ten years of campaigning many of our officers had risked their lives in one battle after another, without ever thinking that they ought to draw up their wills. But they made them now.'[5]

The *Grande Armée* was certainly in a parlous state, lodged deep in central Europe with real or potential enemies on every side. The troops were in desperate need of rest, and the roads through Austria were still thronged with stragglers who were coming to rejoin their units. The force of this depleted army was diminished still further by the need to throw out guards to the strategic flanks and rear. Marmont's II Corps was keeping watch on the Alps, while Davout's III Corps and Mortier's battered VIII Corps were disposed within reach in the area of Vienna. Ney with the little VI Corps was still far distant in Carinthia. So much for the southern flank.

Behind the Brünn position Marshal Bernadotte faced Ferdinand with a combined force of 15,000 Bavarians and French (I Corps). The Guard and Lannes' V Corps formed a central reserve of less than 20,000 troops at Brünn. East of the city facing the main allied army, Napoleon disposed of little more than 30,000 men, namely Murat's cavalry reserve and the IV Corps of Marshal Soult.

Napoleon's one priceless asset was the unique ability of the *Grande Armée* to re-concentrate for combat in instant response to command. If the Emperor was no longer in a position to impose his will on the allies, he could still, by his apparent weakness, tempt them into an offensive move that would betray them in all their clumsiness and lack of co-ordination. This would give him the opportunity for a counter-stroke which could finish the war in a day.

Such was the strategy that was taking shape when Napoleon felt his way over the ground to the east of Brünn in the direction of the allies. On 20 November Murat's cavalry cleared the road junction near Raussnitz, and on the following day Soult and his infantry occupied the country beyond the substantial village of Austerlitz. The cantonments of the French now extended for a good fourteen miles beyond Brünn, and one of their hussar brigades ranged a further five miles to Wischau, which was half way to the position of the main allied army at Olmütz.

Napoleon needed all the warning he could have of any allied move, but what interested him most was the tract of rolling country much nearer Brünn, where he hoped to stage his decisive battle. On 21 November the Emperor visited the advance posts, then rode back to make a careful inspection of his chosen battle-ground. Seven miles short of Brünn he halted at the point where the highway passed hard by the curious mound that later became known as 'the Santon'. The feature was of obvious tactical worth, and he ordered General Claparède to take up position there with the 17th Light. He commanded the eastward slopes to be steeply scarped, and he had between fourteen and twenty light Austrian cannon hauled to the summit and amply stocked with ammunition. He proclaimed that 'if these pieces get off fifty rounds at short range I am quite happy for the Austrians to get them back — they will have earned them. Besides the guns are really theirs.'[6]

Napoleon then turned south and rode from hilltop to hilltop, calculating the distances as he went. On the Pratzen plateau he remarked to his party, 'Take good note of this high ground. You'll be fighting here before two months are out!'[7] To the west a string of villages nestled along a damp valley floor. These too underwent Napoleon's inspection. It was clear that his plans were already being formed, for 'never was any battlefield better examined or better prepared'.[8] Thus when the time finally came to dispose the army for combat Napoleon knew the ground 'as well as the surroundings of Paris'.[9]

What the allies needed most at this juncture was the guidance of somebody like Field-Marshal Daun or one of the other cautious Austrian commanders of the middle of the eighteenth century, who could sense when time was acting on their side, and hold back from any needless encounter with the enemy. Instead, the army was committed to action of the most rash and irresponsible kind.

Arriving at Olmütz on 22 November, Kutuzov was greeted by no less than two Emperors — his own Alexander, and the fugitive Francis of Austria. Alexander had travelled to Moravia by way of Berlin and Silesia. He was confident that he had committed

Prussia to the war, and his self-importance was bolstered by some words of the Austrian minister Cobenzl, who intimated that in critical times it was important for sovereigns to lead armies in person. 'The Tsar believed that these words contained advice and perhaps also a reproach.'[10] Alexander did not wish to deprive Kutuzov of the nominal command—and hence the responsibility for any reverse—but the Tsar and his young friends reserved all the real power for themselves, and they were quick to claim the credit for any success. Once, when Kutuzov asked for Alexander's intentions concerning the movements of the army, he was tartly informed 'that is none of your business'.[11]

The predominant influence was clearly exercised by 'the young gentlemen . . . immediately about the Emperor Alexander'.[12] Orders were now written by Count Lieven, as head of Alexander's field chancery, and transmitted to the army by Prince Volkonsky, who was another of the band of ambitious general-adjutants. Kutuzov withdrew into himself and virtually contracted out of the war.

The Emperor Francis also believed that it was beneath his dignity to oppose the will and resolve of Alexander. In any case the pathetic remnant of the Austrian army was despised by the Russians, who considered themselves the only battleworthy opponents of the French. The one Austrian to retain any influence was Major-General Weyrother, the staff officer who had guided the Russians on their march from Poland, and who had recently taken the place of the much-lamented Schmidt, killed by a musket ball at Dürnstein. Weyrother was brave and intelligent, and got on well with the Russians, but he 'had not that confidence in himself which could enable him to give advice at the headquarters, where the greatest degree of wisdom was requisite'.[13] Devoting himself entirely to Alexander, Weyrother's single ambition was to give practical effect to the Tsar's fantasies.

The debates at Imperial headquarters showed clearly enough where the real power lay. The wiser heads—the foreign minister Czartoryski and the generals Kutuzov, Bagration, Miloradovich, Dokhturov and Langeron—were all for postponing action until time had worked its various wonders. Kutuzov wanted the allies to fall back into the Carpathians. When he was asked where he eventually proposed to fight, he replied 'wherever we will be able to join Bennigsen and the Prussians. The further we entice Napoleon, the weaker he will become, and the greater will be the distance that separates him from his reserves.'[14]

Alexander's entourage found all sorts of reasons for pressing for the more dramatic course. Napoleon seemed to have been taken unawares by the arrival of Buxhöwden's army, and every report confirmed that the French were in a bad way, particularly their cavalry. In contrast the Russians were

> 'in consequence of the reinforcements already arrived, very strong; and formidable, not only from their numbers, but still more from the esprit de corps, courage and spirits with which the Russians are animated—They have, during the whole of the retreat from Braunau to this place in every affair in which they have been engaged, been successful, and have, still notwithstanding the superiority of force with which they have had to contend, the same ideas with respect to their superiority, over the enemy, unimpaired, which they entertained at the time they left Russia.'[15]

Weyrother added that the present position in front of Olmütz was untenable, because of the scarcity of supplies, and that the army must therefore advance in the direction of Brünn. It is difficult to see how he hoped to fare better in a countryside which had already been thoroughly eaten out by the rival armies.

At root, the aggressive party sensed Alexander's desire to try conclusions with Napoleon. 'Tsar Alexander wished to experience and win a battle. He seemed to be confident of a victory that would place him at one stroke above the man who as yet had no equal, let alone a rival on the battlefield.'[16] The final decision to advance was taken on 24 November, in the mood of euphoria induced by the arrival of the Russian Imperial Guard. Not everyone could share in the jubilation. Sir Arthur Paget was aware that the Austrians at least had a few skilful commanders at their disposal, '—all good and experienced officers, but for the other when I reflect that he (Alexander) is to be provided by Kutuzov and Buxhöwden . . . and God knows who, then I own I tremble— nobody knows *exactly* where the French are, or in what force'.[17]

Now that the army was committed to the offensive, Weyrother

explained the strategy in the following terms. The united force of 89,000 men was to be kept together in a block,

> 'and to begin with we shall attempt to win the enemy's right flank, and take up a position which will threaten his communications with Vienna, thereby forcing him to abandon Brünn without a fight and retire behind the Thaya. If this . . . movement does not produce the desired effect, we shall exploit the advantages of our own position and superior forces and launch a decisive attack against his right flank, which will drive him from his ground and throw him back on the Znaym road. Subsequently we shall send strong raiding detachments racing ahead from our left wing, and in concert with the corps of Archduke Ferdinand, who is advancing on Iglau, we shall compel the enemy to retreat through the trackless mountains above Krems.'[18]

A 'disposition' for the move was hurriedly distributed among the generals. The army was supposed to move on 25 November, but the necessary provisions could not be collected before the 26th, and 'when *that* day came, some of the generals had not sufficiently studied their dispositions; and thus, another day was lost'.[19]

The combined mass of 89,000 men finally began its westward march at 8 am on 27 November. The front extended for five miles, and the force was divided into five columns, numbered in order from the north or right. The lead was taken by a powerful force of 33,450 Russian infantry, which comprised the first three columns (the commands of Wimpfen, Langeron and Prebyshevsky) and marched close to the foot of the hills of the Moravian Switzerland. Oddly enough this arrangement would indicate that the first intention of the allies was to turn the French left flank, and not the the right, as had been planned by Weyrother. Lieutenant-General Kollowrath led a force of 22,400 infantry and 3,000 cavalry on a course to the left of the highway, and the plain to the south was swept by a fifth column of 8,500 cavalry. The Russian Major Toll admired the apparent exactitude, order and method with which the Austrian staff officers were able to move such masses of troops. The soldiers actually kept step as they strode across the open fields, and four hours' march was enough to bring them to their destination—the position of Bagration with the advance guard, which had remained immobile at Prödlitz.

The march was resumed on the 28th. Bagration led the way, with the main army swarming behind in the same order as before. The village of Wischau was taken from a small party of Murat's troops, and in the evening the advance guard pressed on to the heights of Raussnitz against token opposition. 'The importance of the affair was greatly exaggerated, and Prince Bagration, as a shrewd kind of man, attributed the success to Prince Dolgoruky. This gentleman had the complete confidence of the Tsar, and Bagration knew that he might prove useful to him.'[20]

Only now did Napoleon become aware that something serious was afoot. In the middle of the afternoon, while he was talking with the Prussian envoy Haugwitz in Brünn, he received a series of reports which indicated that his outpost line was caving in. After dictating his first orders, Napoleon betook himself at about 8 pm to the post house of Posorsitz, where he found the Marshals Murat, Soult and Lannes in a nervous and quarrelsome mood. He was told that the camp fires of an entire army could be seen from Soult's position north of Austerlitz.

Further clarification came from Napoleon's reliable aide General Savary, who had been sent to Olmütz for the ostensible purpose of replying to some peace feelers from the allies, but really to find out what these people were thinking, and to convey the impression that Napoleon was afraid of battle. Tsar Alexander had received Savary with the utmost courtesy, but charged him to carry back a letter addressing Napoleon in the insulting style of 'chief of the French government'. The bellicose manner of Alexander's glittering young entourage confirmed Savary in the conviction that the allies were looking for a fight.

Now began the extraordinarily risky game by which Napoleon invited the enemy to come at him by creating an appearance of weakness, while all the time he consolidated his positions and brought up his reserves to within reach. Too great a show of force would frighten the allies away and leave him as badly off as before, yet he could scarcely allow the enemy to pounce on him before he had gathered his army.

Napoleon accordingly sent Savary to keep up the farce of

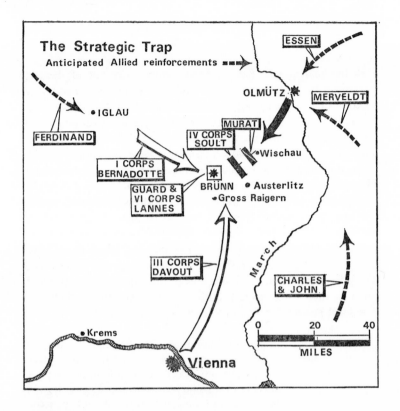

The Strategic Trap

Anticipated Allied reinforcements ■■➤

ESSEN

IGLAU

OLMÜTZ

MERVELDT

FERDINAND

MURAT

IV CORPS
SOULT

Wischau

I CORPS
BERNADOTTE

GUARD &
VI CORPS
LANNES

BRÜNN ● Austerlitz
● Gross Raigern

III CORPS
DAVOUT

March

CHARLES
& JOHN

0   20   40

● Krems

Vienna

MILES

negotiations, and issued the first orders for re-concentrating his
forces. Murat and Soult were to pull back their commands behind
the Goldbach stream. Instructions were sent at the same time for
Bernadotte to come fifty miles from the Bohemian border with the
13,000 French troops of his I Corps, and for Davout's III Corps to
move up from Vienna by forced marches. Thus the bulk of the
Grande Armée drew back to a stronger position, and reinforcements were set in motion from the west and south.

Early in the morning of 29 November the two corps of Murat
and Soult evacuated their positions in the treeless valley around
Austerlitz. The units formed up in a chequerboard formation of
regimental squares, and 'after two hours of marching these thirty
mobile masses stretched over a distance of more than five miles.

The sight was impressive and splendid in the extreme, and the formations sparkled with the reflected sunlight from their weapons.'[21]

With the southern flank at least temporarily out of danger, Napoleon began to devote some attention to his left flank in the region of the highway. He inspected the work on the Santon, and brought up the Guard and the combined grenadier division from Brünn and placed them within supporting distance in the rear. The offices of the Imperial headquarters were established nearby in the dilapidated buildings of the Gandia farm, though Napoleon himself made arrangements to sleep in his coach.

Only now on the 29th did the allies address themselves to the curious discrepancy between the Weyrother strategy, which envisaged a threat against the French right, and the actual formations adopted at the beginning of the advance, which as we have seen, heaped up the main striking force opposite the French left. The allies duly sidled crab-wise four or five miles to the south and piled up their forces to the south of the Olmütz-Brünn highway. The local people watched in horror as

'they trailed through Kutscherau and the neighbourhood from nine in the morning to nine in the evening, like a long chain. They bivouacked . . . in villages and fields, like locusts destroying the corn, and the smoke of their camp fires spread in a dense fog . . . The Russian soldiers are born to endure every kind of oppression and misery, and they are little more than beasts—lumpish, rapacious and insatiable beyond belief. Any object, no matter how heavy, was liable to be tracked down, grabbed and hauled away . . . There was no hole, chest, cellar or lock which was deep or strong enough not to be forcibly uncovered or broken open, and emptied of its contents. The very cradles, cots and babies' clothes were not beneath their attention. And these were our friends, our protectors!'[22]

Bagration with the advance guard pushed in the direction of the Posorsitz post house, but otherwise the forward movement of the host stopped altogether.

Towards midnight Savary escorted one of Alexander's aides-de-camp, the notorious Prince Dolgoruky, to the French outposts on the highway. Napoleon galloped up to hear what he had to say. He tried to keep his temper while the arrogant young Russian conveyed one impossible demand after another, but finally he could contain himself no longer: 'Away with you! Go and tell your master, Monsieur, that I am not in the habit of putting up with insults of this kind. Be gone on the instant!'[23]

After seeing Dolgoruky on his way, Savary rejoined Napoleon who complained to him about the insanity of the Russian demands.

'While he was talking in these terms, he walked back to the first outpost of our infantry – it was furnished by the carabiniers of the 17th Light. The Emperor was angry, and he betrayed his bad temper by lashing with his crop at the clods of earth on the road. The sentry overheard what he was saying. He was an old soldier and he was very much at his ease, filling his pipe while his musket was propped against his legs. Napoleon passed by, and casting a glance in his direction he said "Those Russian buggers think they can make us swallow anything". The veteran immediately joined in the conversation "Not on your life!" he declared, "Not if we have anything to do with it!" The Emperor laughed at these well-chosen phrases. Regaining his composure he mounted horse and returned to headquarters.'[24]

The allies continued to re-shuffle their columns on 30 November. They were short of food, and they moved painfully over bad country tracks in complete ignorance of the whereabouts of the French, who were in fact little more than three miles away. Kutuzov finally established his headquarters at Krzenowitz, while the two sovereigns took up residence at Kirzazowitz, a couple of miles short of Austerlitz.

This respite afforded some relief to Napoleon, who otherwise spent most of the day in a state of anxiety. He was seen 'walking about with his hands joined behind his back – a sign that he was preoccupied with working out some grand scheme'.[25] On the 'allied' side of the Goldbach stream, the French still had their cavalry patrols on the plateau of the Pratzen. Napoleon rode with his marshals to the summit and took in the view, which extended far to the east over the valley of Austerlitz, where the allies were still milling about in some confusion. Everything reinforced the impression that the enemy would ultimately advance over the Pratzen with the intention of turning the French right.

Napoleon proclaimed to the marshals 'I could certainly stop the Russians here, if I held on to this fine position; but that would be just an ordinary battle. I prefer to abandon the ground to them and draw back my right. If they then dare to descend from the heights to take me in my flank, they will surely be beaten without hope of recovery.'[26]

Once the enemy were fully committed in the Goldbach valley, Napoleon intended to fall on the flanks and rear of their salient. Approaching from the south-west, Davout with the III Corps would take the host in the left flank; more important still, the mass of the main army was to debouch from the Santon area to the north, and sweep over the Pratzen plateau, which by now would have been abandoned by the allies. This is what Napoleon had in mind when he dictated the proclamation that was to be read out to the Grande Armée immediately before the battle. Here we find the following sentences: 'The positions which we occupy are formidable, and while the enemy march upon my batteries (i.e. the French centre), they will open their flanks to my attack'.[27]

Napoleon recovered his good spirits towards nightfall, when the re-concentration of his forces at last began to take shape. Bernadotte's I Corps reached the gates of Brünn from the west. Davout arrived in person from the south ahead of his III Corps, which was carrying out the stupendous forced march from Vienna: Gudin's division was still strung out far to the rear, but the fast-moving division of Friant could be expected on the field within twenty-four hours.

The allied army wound out of its bivouacs at eleven on the morning of 1 December, and a couple of hours later the troops began to climb a steepish slope and arrive on the extensive saddleback of the Pratzen plateau. To the French,

'the enemy formation was an impressive sight, as it stood motionless along the crests . . . Their front was covered by *jaeger*, hussars and light artillery. More than two thousand [*sic*] cannon were about to thunder forth. Masses of splendid cavalry appeared in the second line. The front of the Russians stood in the open, and every here and there the green line of their infantry was interrupted by groups of stationary cossacks and regiments of cavalry uniformed in white.'[28]

In reality the columns had become horribly entangled, and darkness descended before the staff officers could discover where all the formations had ended up. The columns were numbered off from left to right (south to north) in accordance with the rearrangement which had taken place since the march of the 27th. The first three columns were strung over the Pratzen in a reasonable approximation to their assigned positions. The fourth column, however, was jammed firmly behind the third. Worse still, the main force of cavalry (the fifth column, under Prince Liechtenstein) had lost its way and bivouacked to the rear of the central columns, far short of where it ought to have been, out to the right near Blasowitz. All of these problems would have to be sorted out on the next morning, which was the day of the great battle.

Napoleon spent the entire day of 1 December on horseback. He toured his army, regiment by regiment and battery by battery, talking to the troops and admonishing the officers. He inspected the field hospitals, and gave instructions to ensure the supply of ammunition from Brünn, which was put in a state of defence. The rival forces now lay within cannon shot, but the troops were more than content to spend the time eating and chatting around the bivouac fires, with their muskets resting harmlessly in piles. Napoleon created the least possible disturbance as he made a leisurely tour of the outpost line from right to left, accompanied by twenty *chasseurs à cheval* of the Guard and a few staff officers. Near the Santon, however, Ségur recalls that an argument broke out as to just how far distant the enemy were. Captain Daumesnil, the commander of the escort, 'was an expert shot, and wishing to show me that the enemy were pretty close, he borrowed a carbine from his men and levelled the barrel over his shoulder. With a single shot he unsaddled a Russian officer who had drawn our attention by the startling whiteness of his uniform.'[29]

Towards three in the afternoon Napoleon repaired to the Zuran

Hill, which lay behind the Santon just to the right of the highway. His grenadiers

> 'had made him a vast round hut on an elevated hillock which commanded a view of the plain. It took the form of a woodman's shelter, with a fire in the middle, and the light entering from the top. Nearby stood the coach in which he had slept the previous nights. The team had been unharnessed. Also close at hand, in the direction of the highway, was an isolated peasant dwelling — the poor cottage where his field kitchen had been established. We (the staff) used to dine with him here in the solitary low room, seated on the benches which were arrayed around one long table.'[30]

Napoleon had been concerned lest the allies should decide to stick fast on the Pratzen. To entice them forward he instructed Murat to stage an apparently panic-stricken retreat with his cavalry, and later in the afternoon he was rewarded by seeing that the enemy were once more on the move. The more the allied deployment became pronounced, the more evident was Napoleon's satisfaction. 'Once or twice he rubbed his hands together in delight. He seemed to be saying to himself: "Now I've got them! They won't escape me this time!" '[31]

The assembly of Napoleon's own troops was proceeding in a satisfactory way. The main force was already heaped up along the axis of the highway: V Corps stood on a rough line with the Santon nearest the enemy; then came the Guard and the combined grenadiers, which were grouped around Napoleon's wooden wigwam on the Zuran; finally the freshly-arrived I Corps under Marshal Bernadotte stood to the rear in the upper Goldbach valley, perfectly screened by the swell of the Zuran.

To the south the IV Corps of Marshal Soult was strung out rather thinly along the Goldbach, in accordance with Napoleon's desire to keep his right centre temptingly weak. At seven in the evening the first of the 3,800 bone-weary men of Friant's division of III Corps stumbled into Gross-Raigern, on the extreme right rear of the field. Coming from Vienna, they had been pushed seventy-six miles in forty-six hours, and only a lavish distribution of wine had given the men the heart to plod on.

2. Pratzen landscape: the view north-westwards from the Pratzeberg, looking over Pratzen village.

3. The view eastwards from the Zuran hill. The Santon is the dark lump in the centre of the horizon; the low hills of the Moravian Switzerland are on the left.

14. Napoleon at the St Anthony Chapel.

Returning to his bivouac, Napoleon distributed the proclamation which he had composed on the day before (see p. 80), and which had been printed on the mobile press which followed headquarters. The sheets were passed by the colonels to the company commanders, who read the text to the men by the light of the bivouac fires:

'Soldiers, the Russian army confronts you with the purpose of avenging the Austrians at Ulm. The Russian battalions are the same which you beat at Schöngrabern, and the same which you have pursued without respite until now. We occupy formidable positions, and while the enemy march upon my batteries, they will open their flanks to my attack.

'Soldiers, I shall direct your battalions in person, I shall hold well back from the fire if, with your customary valour, you throw the enemy lines into disorder and confusion. If, however, the victory appears for a single moment uncertain, you will see your Emperor expose himself in the front ranks. We cannot afford to let victory slip from our grasp on a day like this when the honour of the French infantry and the whole nation is at stake.

'Let no one leave the ranks on the excuse of carrying away the wounded. Let everybody be convinced that we must beat these hirelings of England, who are inspired with such a great hate for our nation.

'This victory will complete our campaign, and we can then resume our winter quarters, where we shall be joined by the new armies which are forming in France. And then the peace which I shall make will be worthy of our people, of you, and of myself.'

CHAPTER 7

GROUND, FORCES AND PLANS

For centuries the tract of open land between Brünn and Austerlitz had known the comings and goings of armies and sovereigns. The fortress-town of Brünn and its grim citadel of Spielberg had helped to save the Austrian monarchy from the Prussians in the last century. At the hamlet of Raussnitz, a dozen miles to the east, the reforming Emperor Joseph II had deigned to descend from his coach and try his hand at a peasant's plough. A pillar was raised to commemorate the event. Joseph's mother, the great Maria Theresa, had been known to visit the tasteful palace at Austerlitz, a short distance to the south, and watch the peasants of Prince Kaunitz perform their country dances.

Now, in December, 1805, all attention was focused on a stretch of this countryside measuring roughly four miles from east to west and nine miles from north to south. The only feature of immediately apparent significance was the northern edge of the field, which was formed by the low wooded hills of the 'Moravian Switzerland', which approached the Olmütz-Brünn highway as it marched from east to west.

The rest of the field is best described with reference to the plateau of Pratzen, which formed an irregular triangle bounded to the north by the highway, to the west by the Goldbach stream and its tributaries, and to the south-east and east by the valleys of the Littawa and its tributary the Raussnitz stream. So famous in military history, the Pratzen presented a surprisingly modest

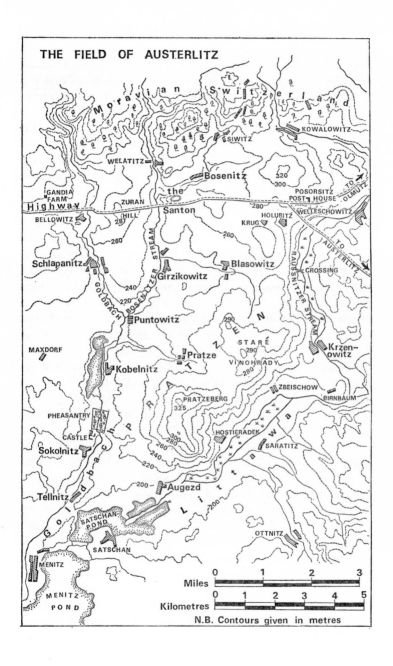

THE FIELD OF AUSTERLITZ

Moravian Switzerland

KOWALOWITZ

SIWITZ

WELATITZ

Bosenitz

320
300

POSORSITZ
POST HOUSE

TO OLMÜTZ

GANDIA FARM

Highway

ZURAN

the

Santon

280

WELLESCHOWITZ

BELLOWITZ

(HILL)
287

HOLUBITZ

KRUG

TO AUSTERLITZ

260

260

CROSSING

Schlapanitz

240

Girzikowitz

Blasowitz

RAUSNITZER STREAM

220

BOSENITZER STREAM

GOLDBACH

Puntowitz

290

Z
E
N

MAXDORF

Kobelnitz

Pratze

STARÉ
290
VINOHRADY
280

Krzen-
owitz

PHEASANTRY

PRATZEBERG
325

ZBEISCHOW

BIRNBAUM

P
R
A
T
Z
E
N

CASTLE

300
280

HOSTIERADEK

SARATITZ

Sokolnitz

240

220

G
o
l
d
b
a
c
h

200

Augezd

L
i
t
t
a
w
a

Tellnitz

200

SATSCHAN
POND

OTTNITZ

SATSCHAN

MENITZ

MENITZ
POND

| Miles | 0 | 1 | 2 | 3 |

| Kilometres | 0 | 1 | 2 | 3 | 4 | 5 |

N.B. Contours given in metres

appearance, being a straggling ridge which only seemed of significance when seen from the marshy level of the Littawa. On the other side, towards the west, the plateau fell away towards the Goldbach and its tributaries in a series of gentle salients and re-entrants. Two villages sheltered in the folds of the hill. One was Blasowitz, just over a mile south of the highway. The other was the hamlet of Pratze, which nestled between the 'high' points of the Staré Vinohrady (298 m, literally 'Old Vineyards') to the north, and the Pratzeberg (325 m) to the south. Except for some vineyards north of the Staré Vinohrady, the Pratzen plateau was open country which offered full access to all arms.

Along the western side of the field, the watercourses of the Goldbach and its tributary the Bosenitzer stream snaked out of Moravian Switzerland and united at the village of Puntowitz. From here the Goldbach wriggled southwards along a damp valley of marshes, thickets and lakes. Along their length the streams were bordered by wretched hamlets of wide muddy streets and single-storey thatched houses. From north to south we number off Bellowitz and Schlapanitz on the upper Goldbach, and Girzikowitz on the Bosenitzer stream. Below the junction at Puntowitz we encounter the hamlet of Kobelnitz, where the Goldbach bordered a long stagnant pond which stretched for about a mile to the south. Below the Kobelnitz pond the stream flowed through the prominent pheasantry or the game park of Sokolnitz—a dark mass of trees and bushes which was enclosed by a low brick wall. The parent castle of Sokolnitz was a solidly-built country house, set about with massive old barns. Further south again, the village of Sokolnitz crowned a muddy bank on the west side of the Goldbach. After nine hundred yards of soggy meadows, one encountered the village of Tellnitz, which stood on the east bank, and formed the last group of habitations before the Goldbach joined the Littawa in a series of wide but shallow fish ponds—the famous 'lakes' of Napoleonic legend.

On 2 December, 1805, the ponds and the stagnant stretches of the watercourses were covered with melting sheets of ice of varying thickness, and in the slight thaw the earthy banks became extremely slippery. The Goldbach line proved all the more effective an obstacle because an observer on the Pratzen could not always see beyond the screen of houses, bushes and orchards.

One feature of the field bulked especially large in Napoleon's plans. This was the prominent hillock (see p. 72) situated beside the highway just east of the point where it crossed the Bosenitzer stream. It was known to the Austrians as the 'Maria-Schneeberg', but the French termed it the 'Santon', for it was crowned with a little chapel which reminded the veterans of the tombs they had seen in Egypt. The Santon rose nearly fifty feet above the surrounding valleys, and gave the French an offensive bridgehead on the far side of the Bosenitzer stream. 'This is what rendered the position so valuable, for it was useful for both defensive and offensive purposes. Master of this position, the Emperor could use it as a base of operations, whether he intended to act in the valley of Bellowitz, that of Puntowitz, or even in that of Blasowitz.'[1]

For the battle of 2 December Napoleon had at his disposal 139 pieces of artillery and a nominal 73–75,000 men. The effective force, however, may well have stood at as little as 60,000, for a sizeable proportion of the establishment was either in no fit state to fight, or fallen by the wayside or had even deserted. We are unlikely to establish the precise figures, for colonels were notoriously unwilling to admit to Napoleon that their units were under-strength.

We shall now enumerate briefly the composition of Napoleon's army from left to right, or north to south (see the detailed description of forces on pp. 181–4). Beginning with the main concentration along the highway, we encounter:

V Corps (Lannes; 12,700 men and 20 guns)
Imperial Guard (Bessières; 5,500 men and 24 guns)
Grenadier division (Oudinot; 5,700 men)
I Corps (Bernadotte; 13,000 men and 24 guns)
Cavalry Reserve Corps (Murat; 7,400 men)

Further south along the Goldbach was positioned the IV Corps (Soult; 23,600 men and 35 guns). Arriving from the direction of Vienna, the III Corps (Davout) could put into the field only the infantry division of Friant (3,800 men and 9 guns) and the supporting dragoon division of Bourcier (2,500 men and 3 guns).

Napoleon's ideas about the coming action underwent a number of subtle changes, and culminated in a final master plan which by no means corresponded with the sequence of the battle as it was actually fought.

What we shall term the 'First Plan' was the Emperor's original design to entice the allies to attack his right centre, and then pinch them out from either side with Davout attacking from the south, and the main army irrupting from the north against the hostile right and rear. As the light faded on 1 December it became increasingly evident that the subsidiary attack from the south was becoming less and less feasible. Not only was it clear that Davout would take the field with little more than a dog-tired remnant of III Corps, but every report indicated that the allies were themselves sliding further and further to the south.

These considerations led Napoleon to formulate his 'Second Plan', which was enshrined in a set of *Dispositions Générales* dictated towards eight in the evening, and supplemented by various verbal orders. Davout was now to make directly from Gross-Raigern to Turas, on the plain behind the Goldbach, with the more modest objectives of expelling any enemy who might have reached that far, and of joining the IV Corps of Marshal Soult, which formed the right wing of the main body. By the same token, the blow of the main body of the *Grande Armée* assumed all the greater importance. As soon as the allied host had descended from the Pratzen heights, the French would launch something like an oblique attack *à la Prusse*, with the right wing taking the lead. Napoleon presupposed that the French would be pushing over ground that had been abandoned by the allies, and so the *Dispositions Générales* were concerned above all with measures of traffic control, designed to prevent the component parts of the mass from getting in one another's way.

According to this 'Second Plan', Soult's IV Corps was to pass swiftly and silently over the valley between Puntowitz and Girzikowitz and win as much terrain as possible on the now empty plateau of Pratzen. The rest of the army stretched in retired echelon to the left—next in line was the mass of cavalry, which was to form in column so as to present the least possible space between the two corps of Soult and Lannes. Oudinot's grenadiers and Bernadotte's I Corps were ordered to press close behind Lannes, and the Guard was to be held in support close by Napoleon's command post on the Zuran Hill.

Having made his dispositions, Napoleon saw no point in waiting around in a state of gloomy apprehension, and so for an hour or so he took his ease at supper with a motley group of commanders and staff—Murat, Junot, Caulaincourt, Mouton, Rapp, Lemarois, Lebrun, Macon, Thiard, Ségur and the surgeon Yvan. Napoleon's meals were usually a hurried affair, but this time he lingered over his fried potatoes and onions (a favourite dish), and he deliberately turned the talk away from the war, as if mocking the apprehensions of the company. In order to bring the well-read Junot into the conversation, he launched into an attack on the modern dramatists: 'But just look at Corneille, and consider his tremendous power of imagination! He ought to have been a statesman!'[2] After a while Napoleon turned in wistful mood to his hopes of an Oriental empire, which had been dashed at Acre in 1799, and he complained that the French did not like to be far from home. Junot ventured to protest, but the brutal old Republican General Mouton broke in to say that no one should be deluded by the present eagerness of the *Grande Armée* for battle. The soldiers just wanted to settle the campaign once and for all, and then go back to France. Napoleon had to agree, and he got up from the table exclaiming 'meanwhile, let's go and fight!'[3] The time was nine in the evening.

Napoleon stretched his legs by making a tour through the bivouacs. He seems to have found everything in order, but he was perturbed by firing to the south, and ordered his staff to investigate. Returning to the Zuran he threw himself down on some bales of straw, and left word that he was to be awakened upon any news of importance. At midnight General Savary galloped back from the right and found Napoleon so fast asleep 'that I had to shake him to wake him up'.[4] Savary reported that the allies had evicted the *tirailleurs de Pô* from Tellnitz, and that they were heaping up considerable forces behind.

The matter demanded further investigation on the spot, and Napoleon called Soult and set out with a small party for the right.

The enemy appeared to have halted their advance, but in attempting to see the line of their watch fires Napoleon ran into a party of cossacks and was chased over the Goldbach. Some of the horses stuck in the mud, and surgeon Yvan had to be extricated by Napoleon's companions.

Napoleon made his way back towards the Zuran on foot, passing among his troops as they huddled around the embers of their fires on this freezing night. He was recognized in the bivouacs of the Guard, whereupon one of the grenadiers took up some straw from his bedding and twisted it into a torch to light him on his way. Within moments the Emperor and his companions were surrounded with troops who shouted with delight and held their improvised torches aloft. Flaming wisps of straw rained down on the scene, and the officers called out in some alarm 'Watch out for your cartridge pouches!'[5] Napoleon was deeply moved, after a little preliminary annoyance at the display.

It took a little time for the rest of the army to awaken to what was happening. Nearby in the bivouacs of Berthier's staff, the younger officers had been enlivened by the arrival of a friend with tidings from France.

> 'Everything was calculated to raise our spirits to the utmost—the news and the little pictures from our families, with perhaps a few love letters . . . the Tokay wine which we sucked from the barrel with straws, the crackling camp fire, and the feeling that we were going to win the battle on the next day. But little by little sleep stole up on us, and the singing died away. Sublimely happy we stretched out under a sky of glittering stars, wrapped in our cloaks and lying on a little straw. We were asleep or already dreaming when suddenly we were aroused by shouts of joy and a blaze of brilliant illumination.'[6]

Napoleon finally returned to the Zuran Hill in a sea of light, and on entering his wigwam he exclaimed, 'this is the finest evening of my life!'[7]

The various impressions of the night strongly indicated that the allies were going to make their main effort even further south along the Goldbach than Napoleon had expected. He responded by formulating his 'Third Plan', a blanket term for the individual

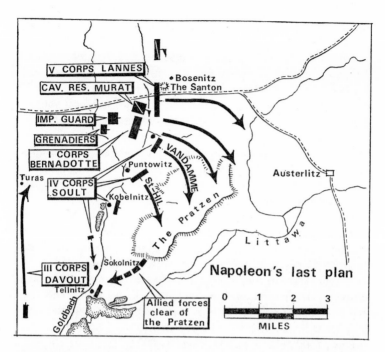

V CORPS LANNES
CAV. RES. MURAT
• Bosenitz
✝ The Santon
IMP. GUARD
GRENADIERS
I CORPS BERNADOTTE
• Puntowitz
VANDAMME
ST.HIL.
Turas
IV CORPS SOULT
Kobelnitz
Austerlitz
The Pratzen
Littawa
III CORPS DAVOUT
Sokolnitz
Tellnitz
Napoleon's last plan
Goldbach
Allied forces clear of the Pratzen
0   1   2   3
MILES

instructions which were issued in the early hours of the morning, and confirmed in the final orders group with the marshals just before the battle.

Essentially a modification of the 'Second Plan', the new scheme teased out the *Grande Armée* a little further to the south, slightly weakening the huge concentration along the axis of the highway.

Soult's IV Corps was the formation most immediately affected. During the night the whole of the 3rd Line had ultimately been committed on the right flank, where it recaptured the village of Tellnitz from a force of Austrian *chevaulégers*. To lend further support in this direction, the 26th Light was ordered to march on Sokolnitz, and the 18th and 75th Line and the Corsican sharp-shooter battalion were positioned in front of Kobelnitz. Most important of all, the entire division of Saint-Hilaire was drawn out of its position in the second line and re-inserted on the right of the main body of IV Corps, ready to pass the Goldbach valley in the neighbourhood of Puntowitz. Thus approximately two-thirds of the corps was strung out along four miles of the lower Goldbach.

Part of the main army was re-shuffled accordingly. Bernadotte's I Corps remained in reserve, but was shifted a few hundred yards further south behind the leftmost division (Vandamme's) of IV Corps. It now became all the more important for Murat with the cavalry reserve to act as a mobile liaison among the elements of the centre. Along the axis of the highway, Lannes was deprived of I Corps' support. This scarcely seemed to matter, for the allied concentration on the southern flank of the field indicated that Lannes and Soult would have a clear sweep across virtually undefended terrain.

Away on the southern flank Davout's depleted III Corps seems to have been almost forgotten. It was only after the battle was already joined that he received orders to bear to the right and reinforce IV Corps in its defence of the lower Goldbach.

Except on the northern flank, the allied arrangements and plans corresponded reasonably well with the picture which had been built up by Napoleon. Tsar Alexander and his nominal commander in chief, Lieutenant-General Kutuzov, had under their orders a total of between 80,000 and 87,000 troops, with 278 pieces of ordnance. At full establishment the Russian contingent should have amounted to something like 62,400 infantry, 12,800 regular cavalry, 6,500 gunners and 4,000 cossacks. However the Russians had lost 5,840 men by direct enemy action during Kutuzov's retreat, not to mention the many sick, deserters and stragglers. Indeed the dozen battalions which had fought at Schöngrabern could muster only some 300 men each. The gunners had been reduced to 5,000, and at the best of times the cossacks were reckoned to be of little use in open battle.

The Austrian element came under the overall command of Lieutenant-General Prince Liechtenstein. The force comprised twenty-and-a-half battalions and forty-five squadrons, which by Stutterheim's calculations came to 15,715 men. Some of the whitecoats were veterans of the Bavarian campaign, burning to avenge the shame of Ulm, but the rest had been hastily raised in the neighbourhood of Vienna from the sweepings of the streets and the alms-houses.

Altogether the rival armies were well matched. If the allies had the crude advantage in numbers, we must also take into account their exhaustion and disunity, the clumsiness of their movements, and their generally low morale—for which the optimistic delusions of Alexander's cronies could offer no real compensation.

For three days now the allied host had manœuvred in open country in the close proximity of the *Grande Armée*. 'They completely ignored the fact that everything on a battlefield comes down to a question of space and time. They seemed to forget that they were dealing with the greatest commander in the world, and they failed to recognize that even his apparently unconsidered actions were the direct reflection of some very deep thinking.'[8] On 1 December the army finally came to rest along the summit and rearward slopes of the Pratzen (see pp. 80–1). The confidence of Weyrother and the Russian staff officers was fed by a reconnaissance carried out by General-Adjutant Prince Dolgoruky, who put the French force with reasonable accuracy at 60,000 men, which was patently inferior to that of the allies. The conduct of the French cavalry and the words of Napoleon himself indicated a generally timorous frame of mind. Moreover the allies had the help of an exact knowledge of the ground, for the Austrians had carried out large-scale manœuvres on the same terrain in 1804. Even after the battle Weyrother was prepared to maintain that 'all the advantages lay on the side of the allied army'. He explained that the French right wing was badly outflanked, and that in retreating north through the valley of the upper Goldbach it should have become entangled with the mass of infantry on the French left, bearing the whole lot away in wild disorder.[9]

In the course of the day Weyrother and his Russian friends, therefore, argued in favour of an offensive designed to turn the French right. The details were to be settled later, but in the evening Alexander and his entourage rode over some of the ground of the proposed march.

'We encountered a detachment of Croats. They were intoning one of those dirge-like and melancholy songs of theirs. The music, the cold and the mist put us in a gloomy mood. Somebody said that tomorrow was a Monday, a day which the Russians consider

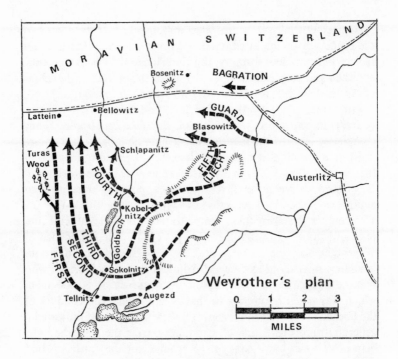

MORAVIAN SWITZERLAND

Bosenitz

BAGRATION

Lattein   Bellowitz

GUARD

Blasowitz

Turas
Wood

Schlapanitz

FOURTH

FIFTH
(LIECHT.)

Austerlitz

Kobel-
nitz

Goldbach

THIRD

SECOND

Sokolnitz

FIRST

Tellnitz   Augezd

Weyrother's plan

0   1   2   3

MILES

unlucky. At that moment the Tsar's horse slipped and fell on a
tussock of grass, and Alexander was thrown from the saddle. The
accident was unimportant in itself, but there were people who took
it as an ill omen.'[10]

However, Prince Dolgoruky's one anxiety was that the *Grande
Armée* might slip away before it came under attack. He betook
himself to Colonel O'Rourke at the advance posts along the
Goldbach, and told him to mark narrowly the direction of any
retreat. On the far right the coming of darkness found Bagration's
leading troops on the hill to the south of Kowalowitz.

'Not far behind the entire army was in bivouacs. To our front we
could see a few enemy fires, which seemed to indicate the line of
their advanced pickets. Everything was silent in the direction of the
hostile army, and we were nearly all convinced that the enemy
were retreating. At about midnight fires suddenly blazed into life

across the foot of the heights on which we were standing,* and we could see their bivouacs extending across a wide stretch of ground. Obviously the enemy were not bothering to conceal their retreat, or so it seemed to many of us. But some people had their doubts.'[11]

This was about the time when the senior commanders were assembling in a spacious room in Kutuzov's headquarters in a peasant house at Krzenowitz. The scene has been set by General Langeron:

'General Weyrother came in. He had an immense map, showing the neighbourhood of Brünn and Austerlitz in the greatest precision and detail. He spread it on the large table, and read his dispositions to us in a loud voice, and with a boastful manner which betrayed smug self-satisfaction. He might have been a form-master reading a lesson to his pupils, though he was far from being a good teacher. We had found Kutuzov half asleep in a chair when we arrived at his house, and by the time we came to leave he had dozed off completely. Buxhöwden was standing. He listened to what was being said, though it must have gone in one ear and out the other. Miloradovich spoke not a word. Prebyshevsky kept in the background, and only Dokhturov examined the map with any attention.'[12]

In brief, Weyrother proposed a 'left-flanking' movement, by which the army would first pass the Goldbach valley on a wide frontage. Having gained the French right, or southern flank, the allies were to pivot on the area of Kobelnitz–Puntowitz and 'throw and pursue'[13] the enemy northwards across the highway and into the wilds of the Moravian Switzerland.

The attack was to be carried out in the same unwieldy mixed columns by which the army had been moving across Moravia in the last few days. The initiative was to be taken by a detachment of Austrians and a main striking force of four columns, numbered in order from the left or south. On the right centre the Russian Imperial Guard was to remain in reserve. Finally on the extreme right the original advance guard under Bagration would hold the highway—a fact which escaped Napoleon's attention.

In detail Weyrother specified that the rôle of left marker was to

* The famous torchlight procession.

be assumed by the Austrian Lieutenant-General Kienmayer, who would force the lower Goldbach with a detachment of five battalions and twenty squadrons of Austrians and two small regiments of cossacks (6,780 men—this figure, like the following figures, presents the over-optimistic nominal establishment). Throughout the advance Kienmayer's job was to stick by the left flank of the first column, covering it from all interference by the enemy.

The first column of the main army consisted of a powerful force of 13,650 Russian infantry commanded by Lieutenant-General Dokhturov. This capable soldier was to gain the Goldbach crossing at Tellnitz, then swing to the right to align himself with the second column. The latter force was made up of 11,700 Russian foot, led by Lieutenant-General Langeron, the French *émigré*. Langeron was to pass the Goldbach between Tellnitz and Sokolnitz, while Lieutenant-General Prebyshevsky's third column (7,700 Russians) seized the castle of Sokolnitz and fanned over the ground behind. All three columns were supposed to come under the general supervision of Lieutenant-General Buxhöwden.

The Generals Kollowrath and Miloradovich jointly commanded an Austro-Russian fourth column of 23,900 infantry, which was to pass the Goldbach to the north of the Kobelnitz pond.

All being well, the allies would be across the Goldbach on a frontage of more than four miles, 'and once the first column has detached four battalions to seize and hold the little wood of Turas, the remainder of the first column, together with the other three columns, will advance between this wood and Schlapanitz and crash into the right flank of the enemy. Three battalions of the fourth column will simultaneously gain the village of Schlapanitz.'[13] The passage of the Goldbach was therefore considered as a mere preliminary to the decisive attack.

The rest of the army would lend support in a variety of ways. Lieutenant-General Johann Liechtenstein was to keep the bulk of the allied cavalry in a fifth column (5,375), and deploy in the neighbourhood of Blasowitz to hold the French cavalry in check, and cover the deployment of the infantry to the south with its horse artillery. To the right rear Grand Duke Constantine was to draw up the Russian Imperial Guard (10,530) behind Blasowitz and Krug, 'and act as a support to Prince Liechtenstein's cavalry and the left wing of Prince Bagration'. The Guard therefore constituted the only effective reserve — a notably small one for such a large army.

On the far right Bagration and the old advance guard of a nominal 13,700 troops were to remain on the defensive, guarding the baggage of the army, and covering the fork where the road to Austerlitz and Hungary branched away from the Brünn-Olmütz highway, 'but as soon as Prince Bagration observes the advance of our left wing, he must attack on his own account and throw back the extreme left wing of the enemy, which by then will be giving way. He must also strive to unite with the remaining columns of our army.'[14]

The fashion among commentators has been to dismiss Weyrother's *Disposition* as a military monstrosity, engendered by eighteenth-century notions of pseudo-scientific warfare. In fact the form of the paper was unexceptionable, and would gain high marks as an operational order in a military academy today. It set out the situation of the enemy clearly enough, it defined the tasks of the columns with the minimum necessary detail, and it concluded with a set of co-ordinating instructions.

With the advantage of hindsight, however, we can detect a number of radical flaws in Weyrother's thinking:

1. He failed to allow for the possibility of the French putting up a fight along the Goldbach, let alone launching a counter-attack.
2. He presupposed that the allied army was capable of acting with precision and *ensemble*.
3. He assumed that his *Disposition* would be transmitted with reasonable speed, and that it would be read by Russian commanders who were capable of following the simplest instructions.

Since the document was drawn up in German, the Russian staff officer Major Toll had first to dash off a translation in Russian before the adjutants could make their copies and bear them to the generals. It was almost three in the morning before Toll could get to work, and the battle had begun before some of the generals had so much as received their copies, 'but this is not all, the plan itself and the resolution to attack the French *was not made known to the Emperor until the very morning,* because it was said, *il sera temps que l'Empereur le sache demain matin*'.[15] The other Emperor, Francis of Austria, did not know what was supposed to have happened until weeks after the action had been fought and lost.

Langeron (according to his own account) told Weyrother that he had made no provision for the danger of the French anticipating him by attacking Pratze village. This sounds very much like wisdom after the event. The only other protest was entered by Bagration, and then in the closed circle of his officers. After receiving a copy of the *Disposition*, he objected to the passive rôle that he had been assigned: 'I don't see why I should stand idly by, and watch the enemy send reinforcements from their left wing to their right.'[16] Bagration was not to know what a vital part he was going to play in the unfolding of the battle, placed as he was in the way of the V Corps hammer blow.

The more typical response among the Russians was one of incomprehension. The xenophobic artillery colonel, Ermolov, recalls seeing General-Adjutant Uvarov return with a plan written on 'several sheets, crowded with difficult names of villages, lakes, streams, and distances and heights. We were not permitted to make a transcription, for the plan had to be read by a good many commanders, and there were very few copies available. I must confess that when I heard it read out, I understood very little of what was intended.'[17]

In the French camp by three in the morning 'there was nothing more to be heard. In one sense it was a lull before the storm, but at the same time our divisions were already gathering in the greatest silence under a clear and freezing sky.'[18] During the next three hours the regiments stumbled through the darkness to their forming-up positions. Napoleon was mounted on one of his favourite Arab horses, and his demeanour was alert and confident. Everywhere the tension was almost tangible.

'On the approach of first light there arose such a dense mist that you could scarcely see ten paces. This gave us time to form up under cover, and our army had been so well trained in the camp of Boulogne that we could count on every soldier having his arms and equipment in good order . . . all over the field the silence was unbroken, and you could scarcely believe that so many troops and so many guns were assembled in so small an area . . .'[19] 'there was something holy about this extraordinary hush, after the mad commotion of the evening before—it was as if we bowed our heads in dignified submission before the will of God. Yet it was also the harbinger of a storm of fury and bloodshed that was to be the making and breaking of empires.'[20]

CHAPTER 8

'A STORM OF FURY AND BLOODSHED', 2 DECEMBER, 1805

I OPENING MOVES

FIRST light found Napoleon on the Zuran Hill, where he had arranged to meet the marshals for a final briefing. He took a hurried breakfast without bothering to sit down, then buckled on his sword and exclaimed to the adjutants, 'And now, gentlemen, let's go and do great things!'[1]

The officers ran to their horses to summon the marshals, and before long all the corps commanders (save Davout) came galloping with their aides-de-camp to the mound. 'Thus was assembled the most formidable collection of men you could imagine. What a wonderful sight! . . . Just consider how many leaders, justly celebrated in their various ways, came together around the most famous commander of ancient or modern history.'[2]

The *Grande Armée* was already formed in column and ready to move, but Napoleon did not wish to declare himself before the allies had committed themselves irrevocably on the lower Goldbach. A lively action was already developing at Tellnitz (see p. 89), and an encouraging report arrived to the effect that the last of the allied troops were descending from the Pratzen, which now seemed open to the French advance. It was about half past seven.

'The Emperor gave the marshals their various instructions, then dispatched them with the command "On your way!" Their heads

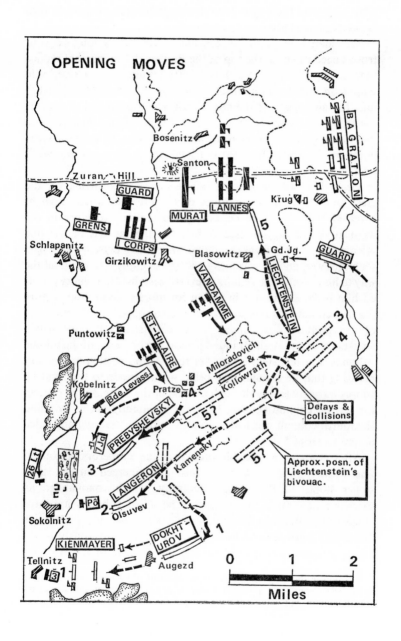

OPENING MOVES

Bosenitz

Santon

Zuran Hill

GUARD

GRENS.

Schlapanitz

I CORPS

Girzikowitz

MURAT

LANNES

Krug

Blasowitz

Gd. Jg.

GUARD

5

LIECHTENSTEIN

VANDAMME

Puntowitz

ST-HILAIRE

3

4

Kobelnitz

Bde. Levass.

Pratze

Miloradovich

&

Kollowrath

2

PREBYSHEVSKY

4

Delays & collisions

26 Lt

3

LANGERON

5?

Kamensky

5?

Approx. posn. of Liechtenstein's bivouac.

Pö

2

Olsuvev

Sokolnitz

1

DOKHT-UROV

KIENMAYER

Tellnitz

3

Augezd

0   1   2

Miles

were high, and their eyes were shining, and each of them in turn saluted and was gone in an instant.'³

Napoleon kept Soult longest, and asked, 'How long do your troops need to get to the top of the Pratzen?' The marshal replied that he required no more than twenty minutes. 'Very well,' said Napoleon, 'we'll wait another quarter of an hour.'⁴ He wished to take full advantage of the heavy mist which promised to conceal the troops for some time yet. After fifteen minutes had elapsed, Napoleon gave the order to depart. Advancing to the best viewpoint on the Zuran he cried out 'One sharp blow and the war's over!'⁵

Meanwhile scenes of some confusion were occurring on the crest and steep rearward slopes of the Pratzen, where daylight revealed that the allied columns were jammed together in the most awkward fashion (see p. 81). On the far left of the line Kienmayer got his little command under way between half past six and seven, and he was lucky enough to enjoy a free run all the way to his objective at Tellnitz. Nevertheless, his punctuality profited him little, for he was in action for more than an hour before the first column (Dokhturov's) arrived to support him. The worst of the muddle was caused by Liechtenstein's cavalry which awakened to find itself stranded behind the bivouacs of the middle columns. Liechtenstein had as yet received no written orders, but realizing that he should have been much further to the right he simply barged his way through the rest of the army. In the process the second column (Langeron's) was apparently cut in two, and the fourth column was forced to wait until the cavalry had trailed across its front.*

After enjoying a passable breakfast, the Emperors Alexander and Francis rode through the mist and emerged on the sunlit upper slopes of the Staré Vinohrady, which commanded an extensive panorama on all sides. The allied columns appeared small and scattered in this intimidating landscape, and the Russian Imperial Guard seemed to be drawing away dangerously to the right. 'Anxiety was plainly written on the face of the Austrian

* However the map to the Austrian *Relation* shows him starting from immediately south-east of Pratze, where he would have got in the way of the fourth column, but could not have severed the second column.

general (evidently Weyrother), and the officers and even the soldiers were troubled as well. Only the gunner officers seemed to be immune from the general depression, having an absolute faith in the efficacy of their pieces.'[6]

In front the troops of the fourth column were standing motionless with unloaded muskets, and Kutuzov was looking on with his sword still in its scabbard. The cavalry had by now cleared out of the way, but Kutuzov, as if paralysed by some presentiment, was reluctant to commit the force to battle. Perhaps the war-weary old Muscovite was reflecting on the apparent uselessness of his troops, twelve battalions of worn-out Russians who had fought under his command on the Danube, and fifteen battalions of Austrians, of which nine had been raised in extreme haste.

Alexander began one of the most famous exchanges in military history: 'Mikhail Larionovich! Why haven't you begun your advance?' 'Your Highness', replied Kutuzov, 'I am waiting for all the columns of the army to get into position.' Alexander retorted, 'But we are not on the Empress's Meadow, where we do not begin a parade until all the regiments are formed up!' 'Your Highness! If I have not begun, it is because we are not on parade, and not on the Empress's Meadow. However, if such be Your Highness's order.'[7] Thus between half past eight and nine, the whole of the left wing of the allied army was finally on the march. The lack of co-ordination was already all too apparent. Lieutenant-Colonel Ermolov explains that,

'the infantry columns consisted of a large number of regiments of foot, unaccompanied by so much as a single cavalryman. Some of the columns therefore had no means of knowing what was going on ahead, or of finding out the location or doings of the neighbouring forces which were supposed to co-operate with them. I myself saw how General Miloradovich begged the commander of a regiment for just twenty hussars to convey vital messages. Not one column owned an advance guard,* and the general advance guard of the whole army (Bagration's command) was on the far right and, in fact, not far ahead of anybody else . . . Thus the columns advanced in false security. Wide intervals yawned between them,

---

* Apart from the first.

for we assumed they would deploy into line of battle on the approach of the enemy.'[8]

By this time the Goldbach valley was reverberating with the noise of combat from the south. The first passage of arms of the whole battle was enacted at about seven far on the allied left, where a few squadrons of Kienmayer's hussars were scouting towards Tellnitz. The little village was situated on the eastern, or 'allied' side of the Goldbach, and it was important for Kienmayer to seize it to open the way for the first column of the main army. The hussars found the prospect unenticing, for the village lurked behind a low ridge, and was set about with little vineyards and orchards that swarmed with French light infantry (*voltigeurs* of the 3rd Line). Away to the left, the Austrians could see a small force of French cavalry (Margaron's command) hovering on the far bank.

Kienmayer responded by throwing in penny-packet attacks of the kind which so attracted Napoleon's scorn. While a regiment of hussars kept watch on either flank, the Austrians committed two waves of infantry from their wild eastern provinces. General Carneville led the way with the 2nd Regiment of Székler Infantry, which pushed into the vineyards to the accompaniment of sounding music and crackling musketry. The troops came under a murderous fire, and before long Kienmayer was forced to commit the remainder of his infantry, namely the 1st Regiment of Széklers and the Broder Croats.

In the course of an hour the Austrians delivered perhaps as many as five attacks, leaving the greater part of the Széklers dead or wounded on the ground. On the French side, the whole burden of the defence rested on the solitary 3rd Line. Its gallant fight indicated how determined the regimental commanders were to dispute the line of the lower Goldbach. Napoleon himself does not seem to have expected the ground to be held for very long.

The 1200 surviving Frenchmen were evicted from Tellnitz only after General Buxhöwden sent a battalion of the 7th *Jaeger* from the first column to support the Austrians in a new attack. Having made his first (and almost his only) intervention in the battle, Buxhöwden was content to occupy Tellnitz and wait for the other columns to come into line.

The sounds of the little battle at Tellnitz attracted the attention of General Legrand, who commanded the right-hand division of Soult's corps at Kobelnitz. He at once took off with the 26th Light and hastened south in the company of General Merle. He had scarcely reached the slope above Sokolnitz when he saw a powerful Russian column descending from the Pratzen. The enemy force was in fact the leading brigade of Langeron's column. The first battalion of the 26th arrived in the nick of time to support the few hundred sharpshooters of the *tirailleurs du Pô*, who until then had been the only forces covering this sector. The second battalion soon pushed in on either side of the first, which brought defenders of Sokolnitz to 1,800 men.

Only now did the third allied column arrive on the scene. Prebyshevsky's force had set off in fine style by way of Pratze village. On the advice of his guides he had then cut across ploughed fields (which can scarcely have speeded his march), and on approaching Sokolnitz he found that French troops were already ensconced in the village and flooding towards the castle. The time was about half past eight. Prebyshevsky had already detached a battalion of the 7th *Jaeger* to safeguard his right flank, and these gentlemen were now assailed by Levasseur's brigade in front of Kobelnitz, and were thrown in some confusion on to the wall of the pheasantry at Sokolnitz. If the Russians wanted their passage at Sokolnitz, they would clearly have to fight their way through.

To the rear, combat was being joined in an entirely unexpected fashion. In Napoleon's thinking the delaying action on the lower Goldbach was entirely subordinate to his plans for the northern sector of the field, where the mass of the *Grande Armée* was to wheel against the open right flank of the allied forces, now apparently committed against the Tellnitz-Sokolnitz line. Soult was to lead the way by directing two of his divisions over the Pratzen plateau, which was seemingly abandoned by the allies.

General Saint-Hilaire's division made up the right-hand half of Soult's striking force, and was in position in front of Puntowitz. The companion division, Vandamme's, stood a few hundred yards to the north-east in front of Girzikowitz. The order had gone out to issue triple rations (almost half a pint) of the gut-busting military brandy, and the troops of Saint-Hilaire's command were further inflamed by the oratory of Soult in person. 'The marshal rode past the regiments, addressing each in turn with that sense of military occasion which he possessed so well. The troops now burst with eagerness and enthusiasm. "Do you remember how you beat the Russians in Switzerland?" he enquired of the 10th Light. Back came the reply "Nobody's likely to forget it today!" '9

While the troops were still waiting 'the sun began to disperse the dense fog. The high ground was the first to clear, and we could see the Pratzen plateau, which was being uncovered by the enemy columns as they marched against our flank. At the foot of the plateau, however, the smoke of the camp fires and the mist still hung heavily over the valley, concealing from the Russians our centre, which was drawn up in columns ready to attack them.'10 Some time after half past eight the two divisions advanced into the mist 'with great coolness, and at a slow pace'.11 At first the battalion columns were closely packed together, but the intervals grew in depth and width when the units began to climb the gentle slopes. At about the 240-metre contour line the troops emerged from the mist into the celebrated sun of the morning of Austerlitz, 'pure and radiant like a perfect spring day'.12 Led by the 10th Light, Saint-Hilaire's division made for the summit of the Pratzeberg, overlooking the church and little streets of Pratze village. Vandamme meanwhile directed his command on the unmistakable outline of the Staré Vinohrady, which rose a mile to the north of Pratze.

Unknown to the French, a substantial allied force was still struggling towards them from the far side of the plateau. By Napoleon's calculations (and Weyrother's own plan) the Pratzen should now have been traversed by all the columns which were making for the Goldbach passages. These logical timetables failed to allow for the chapter of accidents which delayed the march of the fourth column — first the obstruction caused by Liechtenstein's cavalry, and then the paralysing hesitations of General Kutuzov.

It had taken an Imperial command to set the force in motion (see p. 103). The troops were marching in the old-fashioned formation of columns of half-platoons. Lieutenant-Colonel

Monakhtin commanded a small so-called 'advance guard' of three battalions of Russians and a handful of the Austrian Erzherzog Johann Dragoons. Kollowrath and Miloradovich trailed behind with the main body of Austrian and Russian infantry.

Major Toll was sounding the way ahead in the company of a single cossack. As he rode down through Pratze village he espied some troops moving over the ground beyond. He took them for the rearmost elements of Prebyshevsky's column, and he continued confidently on his way until musket balls began to whistle about his ears. Toll galloped back in alarm, and soon the allies came under attack from the front and from the right. Thus was joined the vital battle for the Pratzen plateau.

All the time the French had powerful forces piled in an apparently irresistible mass on the northermost sector of the field. Lannes had the two divisions (Suchet's and Caffarelli's) of his V Corps astride the highway, and he was thickly hedged about with cavalry. Bernadotte's I Corps was making ready to close up in the area of Girzikowitz. Finally the Guard and Oudinot's grenadiers stood in general reserve to the rear.

Here again Napoleon's presuppositions proved to be false. Where he had counted on a clear sweep against the allied right flank and rear, he was in fact confronted by Prince Bagration with the former advance guard of the allies, lurking behind low hills out of the Imperial view.

Bagration had been dissatisfied from the start with the waiting rôle which had been allotted to him by Weyrother's plan (see p. 98). The noise of battle from the south made him more restless still, and towards ten in the morning (the estimates vary greatly) he began to move forward on a wide front, with his three powerful regiments of Russian infantry marching athwart the highway, and hussars and *jaeger* thrown out on the flanks. Lannes' V Corps was set in motion at about the same time, and before long the rival forces could make out their enemies at a distance of a couple of miles.

The one gap in the allied line stretched to the south of Bagration's command, in the sector which was supposed to have been plugged by Liechtenstein's cavalry. Liechtenstein hastened to remedy this, now that he had disentangled himself from the main army. For the sake of speed he had to send his cavalry ahead in two instalments—the main body of 4,000 Russian horse commanded by Generals Uvarov, Essen II and Shepelev, then three regiments of Austrian cuirassiers under Lieutenant-General Hohenlohe. To the rear the Russian Imperial Guard was making its dignified way towards Blasowitz, unaware of the impending drama.

By ten in the morning, therefore, the action was general along most of the seven-mile front of battle. It is useful to take stock of what had happened so far. If everything had unfolded according to the rival plans, the battling forces should by now have been wheeling in a clockwise direction, as each sought to turn the right flank of the other. The powerful French forces on the northern sector were massed together like a stubby hour hand on a dial, pivoting on the area of Puntowitz and making ready to sweep from 'twelve' to 'three'. Conversely the allied columns may be compared with an elongated minute hand, pivoting on the Staré Vinohrady and moving jerkily from 'six' to 'seven'. All too soon the whole machinery jolted to a halt. The movement of the French stuck fast in the presence of enemy forces which, against all expectation, were discovered on the Pratzen and along the highway. The allies suffered much the same experience to the south, where the courageous defenders of Tellnitz and Sokolnitz had jammed the precise mechanism of the Weyrother plan.

For the sake of clarity we shall look in turn at the individual battles that were fought on the Goldbach, on the Pratzen plateau, and in the area of the highway to the north. Lastly we shall witness the defeat of the Russian Imperial Guard, which set in train a sequence of events that drew the hitherto isolated combats together in horrible fashion, and culminated in the rout of the allied army.

II THE STRUGGLE ON THE LOWER GOLDBACH

We left Kienmayer and Dokhturov in possession of Tellnitz, which gave the allies their lowest crossing on the Goldbach. They were not left in peace for long. Up till then the French resistance had been sustained by far-flung elements of Soult's IV Corps. Almost forgotten in all the excitement had been the footsore division of General Friant, which had led the epic march of Davout's III Corps from Vienna, and arrived a few hours earlier at Gross-Raigern. In the process the effective fighting force had been reduced to 3,200.

The leading brigade, that of General Heudelet (108th Line and the *voltigeurs* of the 15th Light) struggled to its feet in the early hours of the morning, and between half past five and six it marched for the village of Turas, where Heudelet was supposed to join the corps of Soult. On the way the brigade was diverted by two messages. The first was an order from Napoleon, which reached Davout at Rebeschowitz and ordered him to make instead for Sokolnitz. On the way thither, word came from General Margaron that Sokolnitz stood in no immediate danger, whereas the 3rd Line was under heavy pressure at Tellnitz. Davout accordingly sent the 1st Dragoons hastening ahead to Tellnitz, with Heudelet's brigade following in their tracks. Jean-Pierre Blaise, a corporal in the 108th Line, recalls that

'when we arrived within cannon shot of the battlefield, we heard a tremendous exchange of musketry between the Russians and the 3rd Line, and we began to encounter a great number of wounded of the latter regiment. At this moment they made us double forward. Thus I was prevented from biting into a leg of goose which I had ready on top of my knapsack. I had intended to eat it there and then, knowing full well that I would scarcely have the leisure later in the day.'[13]

The French bore down on Tellnitz towards nine in the morning. Kienmayer saw them coming, and opened fire with his own guns and those of the first Russian column. 'The discharge of the artillery, together with the continuous fire of musketry, made such a cloud of smoke that you could not see beyond a few paces.'[14] Under cover of the smoke the French burst against the left flank of the battalion of the 7th *Jaeger*, and drove the allies from part of the village. The New Ingermanland Regiment came up to lend support, but merely got entangled with the fugitives in the murk.

While the French *voltigeurs* fanned out in the vineyards, the 108th Line threatened to burst from the eastern exit of Tellnitz. 'However the movement was seen by Colonel Baron Mohr, commander of the Hessen-Homburg Hussars, which was standing in reserve in the rear. He immediately launched an attack, cutting down most of the force of enemy infantry, and scattering the rest.'[15] The Austrian hussars laid about them with all the greater zeal because they mistook the 108th for Bavarians, whom they hated. Kienmayer promptly reoccupied the village with his Austrian infantry and two battalions of the Russians, which had meanwhile been restored to order.

The routed 108th tried to break out to the north along the meadows of the Goldbach, but in the mist and confusion they came under a destructive fire from their comrades of the 26th Light, who were in turn escaping from Sokolnitz. The troops began to recoil into the houses, and the fire ceased only when Captain Livadot of the 108th raised the unmistakable profile of his company eagle.

The two Austrian cavalry regiments now passed through Tellnitz without opposition and formed up on the west side of the Goldbach in line of battle. The first line of Dokhturov's column positioned itself behind, and the second took its place on the east bank. Bourcier brought up his dragoon division in some haste from Gross-Raigern to contain the allied breakthrough, but the Austrians and Russians were content to stand where they were and await the progress of the second and third columns against Sokolnitz.

An exceptionally hot fight was now in progress at the latter village, where the 26th Light had arrived just minutes before the Russian columns began to converge on the scene (see p. 105). Langeron was anxious to keep the second column in line with the rest of the army, and orientating himself on the head of the first column to his left he reached the Goldbach opposite Sokolnitz at about half past eight. Since Prebyshevsky and the third column had not yet put in an appearance on the right, he was content to line up his *jaeger* and his thirty-odd guns and pepper Sokolnitz with musketry, canister and roundshot. Colonel Pouget of the 26th Light describes how he was

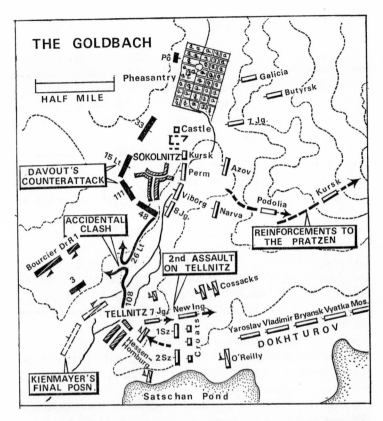

THE GOLDBACH

HALF MILE

Pheasantry

Pő

Galicia

Butyrsk

7 Jg.

□ Castle

ⵏ·7

SOKOLNITZ □ Kursk

33

15 Lt

DAVOUT'S
COUNTERATTACK

Perm

Azov

111

Viborg

Narva

Podolia

Kursk

REINFORCEMENTS TO
THE PRATZEN

ACCIDENTAL
CLASH

48

8 Jg.

26 Lt

Bourcier DrR 1

3

108

2nd ASSAULT
ON TELLNITZ

Cossacks

TELLNITZ 7 Jg. New Ing.

Croats

Yaroslav Vladimir Bryansk Vyatka Mos.

1Sz

Hessen-
Homburg

2 Sz

O'Reilly

D O K H T U R O V

KIENMAYER'S
FINAL POSN.

Satschan Pond

'much annoyed . . . at the restlessness of my horse, which was
startled by the bullets as they whistled around its ears and between
its legs, and prevented me from going to where I knew I was needed.
Major Brillat offered me his own horse, which I eagerly accepted.
At the instant I dismounted I was engulfed in a shower of earth
and pebbles, which flew into my face with such force that I was
covered in blood and almost blinded.'[16]

On arriving opposite Sokolnitz castle and the northern part of
the village (see p. 105), Prebyskevsky could see that he would have
to make his passage by force. He accordingly instructed his
command to 'form dense columns by platoons and regiments, so
as to facilitate whatever movements might prove necessary'.[17]

Major-General Müller III went ahead with two battalions of the 7th *Jaeger* and the Galicia Regiment, and he cleared the extensive castle buildings in short order. The defenders rallied with their guns on a gentle hill to the rear, and Müller was wounded when the battle flared up anew. Major-General Strik promptly took over the command, and drove the French back with the support of the Narva and Butyrsk regiments, which came through the castle compound to help him.

Some of these troops were diverted to the left into Sokolnitz to open a communication with Langeron, who was assailing the village on its southern flank. Langeron committed about 5,000 men to the assault, namely the 8th *Jaeger*, the regiments of Viborg and Perm, and one battalion of the regiment of Kursk. Still battling to hold the village, a large part of the 26th Light was therefore trapped between Prebyshevsky and Langeron. The French lost one hundred men as prisoners as they fought their way to the rear, and they had to abandon two of their guns on the hill behind the village. The rest of the 26th was cut off to the south of Sokolnitz, and in seeking to escape towards Tellnitz the troops collided with the fugitives of the 108th Line (see p. 110).

Sokolnitz village seemed to have been cleared for good, and the leading elements of the two Russian columns pressed through the streets, mingling in some confusion. To the rear a number of mysterious movements were taking place on the Pratzen, and as a precautionary measure Prebyshevsky ordered Lieutenant-General Wimpfen to remain in reserve on the east side of the Goldbach with the Podolia, Azov and Narva Regiments and observe what was happening behind. However the combat at Sokolnitz was very far from complete.

Having been forced to wage a miniature battle to clear a single French regiment from Sokolnitz, the allies were hard put to it to hold their ground when, after ten o'clock, the veteran General Friant threw in the second and third brigades of his division (Lochet's and Kister's). General Lochet in person led the 48th Line in a furious attack which swept over the hill in front of the village and penetrated some way into the streets. Two colours and six pieces were taken in the process. The 111th Line, the remaining regiment of Lochet's brigade, arrived to lend support a little further to the north, and drove back 'a huge mass of leaderless men who were advancing in disorder and uttering horrible cries'.[18]

The Russians returned to the attack, driving the 111th away, and containing the 48th in the southern part of the village, where the troops held out for three-quarters of an hour in the houses and barns. In an attempt to disengage the 48th, Friant now fed in the two regiments of Kister's brigade on the left. The conscripts of the 15th Light fought with unexpected bravery, and broke into the north-western angle of the village. During the combat Sergeant-Majors Broudes and Deschamps 'had to defend their eagles against several Russian NCOs and grenadiers who were doing their level best to seize them. These two heroes each knocked down a number of the enemy by the weight of their eagles, and thus managed to save these standards for their regiment'.[19] Just to their left their companions of the 33rd Line advanced boldly into the patch of ground between the village and the castle.

The vastly superior Russians counter-attacked at every point, but were never able to evict the 48th from its toehold in the south, or to break through the light screen of French forces which hung about the village on the other sides. Thus by the early afternoon the main allied striking force of three columns, or about 33,000 men in all, was still jammed against the lower Goldbach well short of its objectives. Meanwhile events on the Pratzen were already turning the battle decisively to Napoleon's advantage.

III THE BATTLE ON THE PRATZEN

We return to the totally unexpected collision between the divisions of Saint-Hilaire and Vandamme, the spearhead of the *Grande Armée*, and the Austro-Russian fourth column as it toiled over the Pratzen plateau. The allied 'advance guard' (a party of Erzherzog Johann Dragoons, two battalions of the Novgorod Musketeers and a battalion of the Apsheron Musketeers) was still descending towards Pratze village when Major Toll galloped back to give his warning. With commendable speed the leading infantry rushed through the village and over the bridge which crossed a steep-banked stream beyond. The French skirmishers gave way, and

General Miloradovich sent one battalion of the Novgorod Regiment to hold the height south of Pratze, and posted the other immediately outside the village, lying flat on the bank above the stream. Two guns closed up the right flank.

News of the encounter was rushed to Kutuzov and Alexander on the Staré Vinohrady, who could now see for themselves that French columns were ready to advance along the whole central and northern sectors of the field. The Austrian staff colonel Baron Wimpfen at once appreciated the danger to the rear of the first three allied columns, and pointed out 'that our most important objective must be to win the heights to the left of Pratze and occupy them as rapidly as possible'.[20]

Kutuzov accordingly split the fourth column in two. The leading element, consisting of the main body of the Austrian infantry under Kollowrath, was to hasten ahead and gain the summit of the Pratzeberg, south of Pratze village. Miloradovich with the advance guard and the remaining battalions of the first line was to commit his troops in Pratze village and over the Staré Vinohrady to the north. Miloradovich was certainly ready to put on a tremendous show for the Tsar's benefit:

'He was mounted on a splendid English horse with a handy turn of speed. He galloped back and forth along the front, maintaining a high velocity amid all the bullets and shot. He yelled, swore and grumbled at the soldiers, and always positioned himself between them and the enemy.'[21]

Thus the fourth column was teased into a straggling line, with Kollowrath arriving squarely in the path of Saint-Hilaire's advance, and Miloradovich getting involved in Vandamme's as well.

Meanwhile Saint-Hilaire's division was tramping up the gentle incline. The 10th Light led the way under the command of General Morand, a reliable but limited officer with a notably small head. General Thiébault came up behind with his brigade of three battalions. Thiébault had been told that he could expect to encounter no more than a chain of allied outposts on the Pratzeberg, but he had the foresight to keep his forces in line of columns, ready to support Morand as necessary. Only the first battalion of

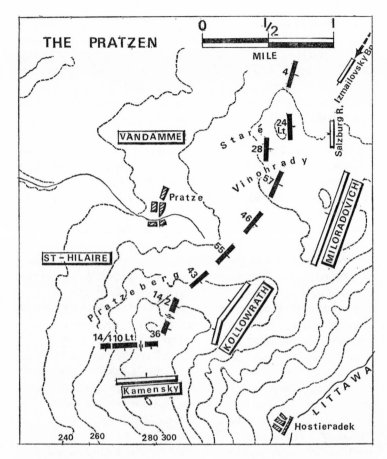

THE PRATZEN

the 14th Line was detached under Colonel Mazas for the purpose of sweeping Pratze village.

The Russians actually got the better of the first clash of arms. On their right the first Novgorod battalion at Pratze stood up at the instant when Colonel Mazas came to a halt at the stream, and poured in a destructive volley at point-blank range. The main body of the Russian line came into action almost at the same time, and Captain Morozov twice led the Little Russia Grenadiers and the grenadier battalion of the Apsheron regiment to the attack with the bayonet, and overran two French guns.

Thiébault was soon at hand to restore order. He pointed the 36th Line at the village, with the second battalion of the 14th Line to its left, and ordered the three battalions to attack without more ado. The French deployed at the run, and they swept across the stream and through the village with such *élan* that the Novgorod battalions gave way and carried the Apsheron grenadiers with them in their flight.

In these horrible minutes Generals Repninski and Berg were wounded and rendered *hors de combat*. The fugitives fled past Alexander regardless of his exhortations, and while he was trying to stay the flight Kutuzov was grazed in the cheek by a musket shot. The Tsar sent his physician, Dr James Wylie, to tend him. 'Would you thank His Highness,' Kutuzov told Wylie, 'and assure him that I am not badly wounded.' Then, indicating the French breakthrough, he added, 'that's where we're really hurt!'[22] Kutuzov continued to give orders until the French were so close that he could see their faces. Finally he made off to the left to Kollowrath's command, his face streaming with blood.

To the south, the height of the Pratzeberg was still very much disputed ground. Here too we can trace the apparently endless consequences of Lichtenstein's passage through the army (see p. 102). Just as the fourth column was delayed by the cavalry in its march over the Pratzen, so the second column (Langeron's) seems to have been cut in two and the rearmost brigade held back from descending from Sokolnitz. This force consisted of the Fanagoria Grenadiers and the Ryazan Musketeers, commanded by General Kamensky I. The general had still not reached the plain of the lower Goldbach when he looked around and saw French columns pouring over the Pratzen. He at once turned the two regiments about and led them back up the slope against the right flank of Saint-Hilaire's breakthrough. The enterprising Russians flooded around the 10th Light, and Morand's little command was saved from destruction only when Saint-Hilaire in person brought up the first battalion of the 14th Line at the run and inserted it on the right.

The French enjoyed only a short respite before Thiébault became aware that a number of unidentified regiments were bearing down on his brigade from the other side, the east.

'When I saw them I halted my three remaining battalions... General Saint-Hilaire rejoined me, and we took up our telescopes to examine the masses that were coming towards us. Nothing seemed to indicate that they were hostile. Soon we could hear their music, and a little later one of their officers came up to extreme shouting distance and called out at the top of his voice "Don't shoot! We're Bavarians!" He returned to his regiments, as soon as he was satisfied we had heard him. "What are we going to do now?" General Saint-Hilaire asked. "General!" I exclaimed "I've got my doubts about these Bavarians. I'm still more suspicious about that officer. After all, he didn't dare to come up to us." '[23]

As a precautionary measure Thiébault shook the entire brigade into a single line and bent it at right angles, so that the right-hand arm faced south towards Kamensky, and the eastern arm confronted the newcomers. In the process the 36th Line was brought up to cover Morand's left and form the angle, while the second battalion of the 14th Line was positioned on the left of the line. At this juncture six 12-pounder cannon—the entire artillery reserve of IV Corps—arrived at the direct command of Marshal Soult. These powerful pieces were placed on either flank of the 36th Line.

Still unsure as to the identity of the sinister regiments to the east Thiébault crawled forward to reconnoitre at closer range. He lighted upon Morand, who was engaged on the same errand. All their doubts were removed when an officer detached himself from Kamensky's brigade and held a brief conference with a counterpart from the strange force. Thiébault and Morand hastened back to their regiments, now certain that they were going to come under attack from two directions.

The hostile units were in fact the two brigades of the Austrian generals Jurczik and Rottermund.

'Judging by the composition of these forces, you would have put very little reliance on them. The men were drawn from the two extremes of military uselessness—namely invalids, and the totally untrained recruits of the sixth battalions.'[24]

In the event this unpromising material fought with surprising vigour, for Weyrother and a sizeable gaggle of staff officers were at hand to lend help, and the presence of Kutuzov put the Austrians on their mettle.

The French guns were loaded with superimposed canister and shot, ready to open fire at a little more than one hundred paces, and the musketeers aimed at the belts of the advancing troops. Thiébault describes how he

> 'allowed these formidable masses to approach to within the predetermined range, whereupon I unmasked my nine cannon and my whole line of battle opened an extraordinarily destructive fire . . . You can imagine how pleased I was when every discharge from my cannon opened great square holes in the enemy lines, and when their four regiments dispersed in mobs of fugitives.'[25]

According to the Austrian account, however, their first attack reduced the French to fighting in open order, and two French officers actually came out to parley.[26] The apparent invitation was not taken up, since the battle was already raging very hotly, and the Austrians suspected that the enemy were playing for time.[27] The French survived only because they made such good use of ground, and because in their dark uniforms they looked so much like Russians that the Austrian gunners hesitated to open fire.

To the allies it seemed that

> 'Only a general attack with the bayonet could decide the possession of the summit, and thus enable us to exploit the advantages we had already gained. To this end the Austrian infantry and Kamensky's brigade joined up, and launched an attack on a wide front. The Russians came on with their usual battle cries, but the French met them with a powerful and sustained musketry fire, which worked to deadly effect in the compact ranks of the allied infantry. The impetus of the first onrush was reduced to a slow advance, supported by musketry. However the courage of the troops was hardened by the exhortations and personal example of the generals and all the other staff officers. Thus the French were forced to give way, and the heroic Russian brigade and the attached battalions of the Austrians . . . were led to the summit of the heights.'[28]

In this supreme effort Jurczik was severely wounded, and Weyrother had his horse shot from under him. Particular credit was earned by Prince Volkonsky (Alexander's future chief of staff) who three times led the Fanagoria Grenadiers to the attack.

On the French side Saint-Hilaire proposed to his brigade commanders that they ought to withdraw to some more tenable position. On hearing these words Colonel Pouset of the 10th Light burst into the group with one bound of his horse and cried out, 'General, don't pull us back! . . . Retreat one step, and we're destroyed. There's only one honourable way out—go bald-headed at whoever is in front of us, and above all don't give the enemy time to see just how few we are!'[29] The French therefore held their ground, and half an hour of assaults by the yelling Russians failed to dislodge them from the Pratzeberg. 'In these terrible encounters, whole battalions of Russians got themselves killed without a single man leaving the ranks. Their bodies were left in the same alignment as their parent battalions.'[30] On specific orders the French bayoneted the wounded without mercy.

Down in the plain of the Goldbach the commander of the allied second column, Lieutenant-General Langeron, had refused to credit a report to the effect that French forces had been seen on the Pratzen. He was sure that the troops must be Austrians, though he could not imagine why they were going in that direction. Almost immediately word came from Kamensky, confirming that the French indeed had powerful forces on the Pratzen. Langeron rode up the plateau in person and reached Kamensky's brigade while it was still engaged against the French at a range of 200 paces. The Russian troops replied to the scourging of canister and musketry with a slow and inaccurate fire.

> 'The troops had fought on for almost two hours, which is all the more admirable when you consider that they were unaccustomed to warfare, that they had been attacked by surprise in the rear, and that they must have been shrinking from the noise of the cannon, which many of them must have heard for the first time.'[31]

Langeron returned to the plain and took personal command of the two unengaged battalions of the Kursk Regiment, which were the first troops he could find. He climbed the slope with the little band, and arrived at the top after Kamensky had finally been broken. The supporting regiment of Podolia was still lagging behind, and so the regiment of Kursk received the undivided attention of the French. Saint-Hilaire took the Russians in front, while the brigade of Levasseur, which had meanwhile come up from the plain, fell on their flank. The regiment was overwhelmed in a matter of minutes, losing 1,600 men and its colours and guns, whilst the Podolia Regiment was pushed back to the Sokolnitz pheasantry.

Langeron escaped from the massacre and rode once more down the slope, this time to inform Buxhöwden, whom he found immobile on a mound south-east of Sokolnitz.

> 'His face was flushed, and it seemed to me that he was no longer in possession of his wits or senses. I told him what had happened on the Pratzen, and that we had been turned and surrounded by the enemy. He replied rather rudely: "My dear general, you appear to see enemies all over the place." I was disrespectful enough to rejoin: "And you, *monsieur le comte*, are in no state to see the enemy anywhere!" '[32]

Thus the allies had now irrevocably lost the Pratzeberg, together with most of their artillery, 'which was entangled in the deep clay that prevails in that part of the country'.[33]

Meanwhile the peppery General Vandamme had gained a rapid and apparently decisive success over the allies on the Staré Vinohrady, the northern prolongation of the Pratzen. Like his counterpart Saint-Hilaire to the south, he thinned out his division in a single frontage, placing the brigade of Férey in the centre, and moving the brigades of Varé and Schinner respectively up to the right and left.

In his first push Vandamme helped Saint-Hilaire to dispose of Miloradovich's Russians (see p. 114). However at the rear, or right of the allied column, the powerful Austrian regiment of Salzburg escaped relatively unscathed, and it clung stubbornly on to the Staré Vinohrady until Vandamme was compelled to put in a concerted attack by Férey's brigade, supported by the 55th Line to the right, and Schinner's brigade to the left. Only now were the gallant whitecoats pushed off the dominating feature, having suffered a significantly high proportion of casualties at close range.

This was the virtual end of the allied fourth column. In the words of Miloradovich, 'up till then the troops had put up a stubborn fight. But now the cumulative effect of the catastrophic situation, their own exhaustion, the lack of cartridges, the disadvantageous lie of the land, and the enemy fire which came in from every side, all made them give way in disorder.'[34]

Vandamme's hold on the plateau was soon to be challenged by no less an opponent than the Russian Imperial Guard. All the same, he and Saint-Hilaire had thoroughly cleared the fourth column from this vital ground. More important still, they had virtually destroyed the central direction of the allied army.

General Kutuzov had been caught up in succession with the little battles of Miloradovich and Kollowrath. He ended the day with Kamensky's brigade, and retired with it to Hostieradek in the Littawa valley. After the battle he had to confess that he was not able to report on the conduct of the officers, 'since my location on that day did not permit me to see in person what was happening elsewhere on the field'.[35]

Alexander was separated from Kutuzov in the first confusion around the Staré Vinohrady. His ministers and courtiers disappeared like smoke, and the glittering generals and aides melted away on various errands, leaving him in the company of his physician Wylie, two mounted attendants and two cossacks. The Tsar was now powerless to influence the course of events, except perhaps by showing an example of courage in what was his first battle. A howitzer shell was seen to explode a short distance to his rear, and at another moment a shot ploughed into the ground just two paces in front of him, covering him with earth. We shall catch only one more glimpse of Alexander before he departs from the field.

In contrast with the disruption in the allied command, Napoleon kept himself thoroughly conversant with what was going on. He spent the first hours on the Zuran hill, which gave him a view of a wide sweep of the field from the Moravian Switzerland to the summit of the Pratzeberg. He 'showed extreme composure throughout the battle, and the stony calm of his face hardly altered for a second'.[36] Every now and then he received details of one or another of the actions from couriers who came galloping up on sweating horses. He sent the appropriate orders back, after consulting a sheet of paper on which were entered the names of all the divisions and brigades.

Napoleon lost sight of developments in the centre once Vandamme had crowned the Staré Vinohrady. Moreover the sky was beginning to cloud over, and some time after eleven he rode forward on his little Arab horse to gain the summit. Almost the whole reserve advanced with him to occupy the ground which had been won, namely the cavalry and infantry of the Guard, Oudinot's grenadiers and Bernadotte's I Corps.

Napoleon had chosen Ségur to carry the appropriate orders to Bernadotte, with the special commission to see that they were actually carried out. Ségur found that the marshal was 'disturbed and anxious. He had told his troops to be calm, but he was setting a pretty bad example.'[37] As Napoleon half expected, Bernadotte got his corps on the move only under protest.

There was no hesitation about the advance of the Imperial Guard. It marched by closed divisional columns, in 'full parade uniform, with bearskin caps and plumes flying in the wind, and uncased eagles and pennons . . . in this order we crossed the plain and climbed the far heights to cries of *Vive l'Empereur!*'[38]

The musicians were present in full force at the centre of each battalion, and Grenadier Coignet admired the performance of his own chief bandsman,

'an old campaigner of at least sixty. They were playing a song we knew very well:

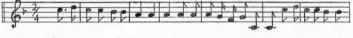

On va leur percer le flan Et flin flan r'lan tan plan tire lire en plan On va leur percer le

flan Ah!que nous allons ri..re Ah!que nous allons ri..re r'lan tan plan tire lire Que le ciel sera con-

tent En plein plan r'lan tan plan tire lire en plan Que le ciel sera content On fait ce qu'il désire

122

As a form of accompaniment, the drummers under their drum-major Sénot beat the charge fit to burst their instruments. The drumming and the music intermingled, and the effect was enough to galvanize a paralytic.'[39]

Napoleon arrived at the Staré Vinohrady in time to witness the dramatic 'attack' of the Russian Imperial Guard, which threatened to disrupt the whole development of the battle (see p. 135). By now, however, we have run ahead of our story. We must first turn to the events on the far northern flank of the field, where Bagration and Lannes were waging a bitter, private war.

IV BAGRATION'S BATTLE

We last saw the rival forces of Bagration and the V Corps as they advanced towards one another along the axis of the highway, while Liechtenstein's cavalry came hastening over the plateau from the south to lend help to the Russians.

Liechtenstein opened a heavy fire from the batteries of horse and reserve artillery which he had brought with him, and he did what he could to deploy the cavalry over the dangerous gap which separated Bagration's force from the main allied army. To Liechtenstein's left or rear, Lieutenant-General Hohenlohe detached the Austrian cuirassier regiment of Lothringen in the direction of the Staré Vinohrady, where sinister movements were already to be seen. In his centre the battalion of Guard *Jaeger* came up from the reserve to occupy the village of Blasowitz (see p. 133). Finally the main body of about 4,000 Russian horse held straight on and launched a spoiling attack against Lannes' corps and the supporting cavalry. Almost immediately, however, the Russians were 'thrown back by a salvo of canister, murderously supported by the musketry of the enemy foot and the carbines of their cavalry'.[40]

It took the combined efforts of Generals Uvarov and Essen to restore the shaken regiments to order and prepare a new attack. This good work was largely frustrated by the impetuosity of the

Grand Duke Constantine Uhlans, who threw themselves without support against the front and right flank of Kellermann's division of light cavalry. The French horse scattered in a gratifying fashion, but when the lancers closed with the enemy infantry they met a rolling fire at point blank range. They rampaged along the front of the infantry divisions of Caffarelli and Suchet from one end to the other, meeting fire all the way, and finally disappeared along the highway. The regiment lost 400 men in the process, and its commander Müller-Zakomelsky fell into the hands of the French, together with sixteen of the officers.

Now that he was free of the lancers, Kellermann advanced the left-hand regiments of his division. This immediately provoked a series of counter-attacks on the part of the Russian cavalry, which (according to French accounts) descended upon Kellermann and Caffarelli in overwhelming force.

> 'At this juncture you could appreciate just how much military training and experience can affect the course of an action. The troops of Caffarelli's division . . . opened up their intervals as coolly as if they had been on a parade ground. Immediately Kellermann's cavalry passed through they closed up again and opened fire on the enemy.'[41]

Kellermann moved forward once more, only to be assailed by the Pavlograd Hussars and the Tver and St Petersburg Dragoons, which had been lurking behind Bagration's infantry. This was probably the scene witnessed by a French lieutenant of horse artillery, who describes how he suddenly found the Russian cavalry surging around his guns:

> 'The soldiers threw themselves beneath the ammunition carts and the pieces, while the gunners defended themselves with their rammers. For a time the infantry was unable to shoot, because the mass of Kellermann's cavalry stood in the way, but once the field was clear they opened a rolling fire at thirty paces. At that moment I was at bay among my draught-horses, fighting hand to hand with a Russian officer. He had severed the little finger of my right hand with a blow of his sword, but all at once his horse collapsed, struck by a musket ball. The officer cast himself at my stirrups and

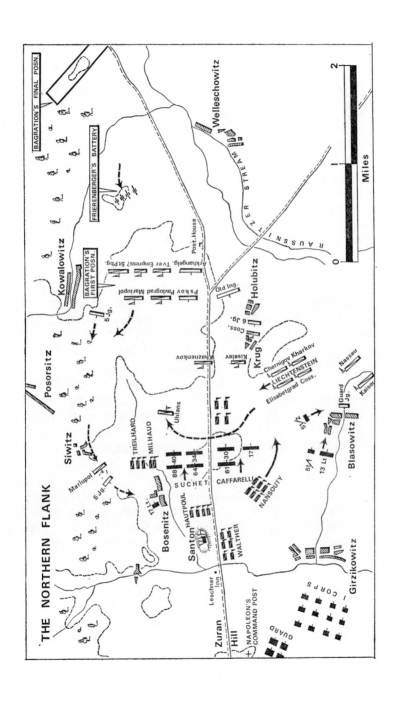

THE NORTHERN FLANK

BAGRATION'S FINAL POSN.

FRIERENBERGER'S BATTERY

Kowalowitz

BAGRATION'S FIRST POSN.

5 Jg.

Posorsitz

Siwitz

Mariupol

5 Jg.

Bosenitz

17 Lt.

TREILHARD

MILHAUD

Uhlans

88 40

64 34

SUCHET

HAUTPOUL

Santon

WALTHER

Leschner Inn

Zuran Hill

NAPOLEON'S COMMAND POST

GUARD

I CORPS

Girzikowitz

Welleschowitz

ZER STREAM

RAUSSNITZ

Post House

Arkhangel. Tver Empress' Stpb.

Pskov Pavlograd Mariupol

Old Ing.

Holubitz

6 Jg.

Coss.

Kiselev

Krug

Khaznenkov

Chernigov Kharkov

LIECHTENSTEIN

Elisabetgrad Coss.

Nassau

Kaiser

Guard Jg.

5/2

5/1

61 30

17

CAFFARELLI

NANSOUTY

5/1

13 Lt.

Blasowitz

Miles

0   1   2

cried out, "We are heroes after all, aren't we?" He repeated these words several times and kept by my side, regarding himself as my prisoner.'[42]

Murat himself was caught up in the fighting, and for a time he and his staff had to hack about them with their sabres. Only the intervention of the heavy cavalry division of Nansouty could possibly restore the balance. This formidable body was brought out of its reserve position behind V Corps and fed into the battle on the southern flank of Caffarelli's division.

The brigade of carabiniers was the first into action. They braved a destructive fire from Russian artillery, and then, when Nansouty judged they had come sufficiently near he ordered *au trot* and immediately afterwards sounded the charge, 'which was carried out with such precision and co-ordination that you might have thought they were drilling in front of an inspector general'.[43] The noise of the clash was heard all over the field. The first line of allied horse crumbled, whereupon the 2nd and 3rd Cuirassiers came up to help their unarmoured brothers in the carabiniers to overthrow the head of Liechtenstein's column, which was formed of the Elisabetgrad Hussars and the Chernigov Dragoons.

Nansouty recalled his victorious command to draw breath behind the infantry. However the 3rd Cuirassiers experienced some difficulty in extricating themselves, and Liechtenstein seized the chance to throw himself once more on the exposed right flank of Caffarelli's infantry. Without attempting to form square the French troops held Liechtenstein back with blasts of musketry until Nansouty once more appeared in their support.

This time Nansouty formed his division in two parallel columns of platoons, and fed them through the gaps in the infantry at a fast trot. The troopers thereupon deployed in front of Caffarelli, with the carabinier brigade and the 2nd Cuirassiers in the first line, and the 3rd, 9th and 12th Cuirassiers in the rear. The French rolled forward, and the weight of their cuirassiers once more proved decisive in the *mêlée*. The offensive power of Liechtenstein's cavalry was now badly weakened.

Events had also taken an unfavourable turn just to the south in the area of Blasowitz. In that part of the world Liechtenstein had a battery of horse artillery and the two uncommitted regiments of Austrian cuirassiers. They lent support to the Russian Guard *Jaeger* in the village, and helped to fill the void which still yawned between Bagration and the fourth column. At about half past ten Lannes sent forward the 13th Light and the first battalion of the 51st Line to clear the ill-assorted allied force out of the way. Four companies of the 13th Light accordingly advanced in skirmishing order, but were promptly repelled by the *jaeger*.

If we believe the French accounts, the defenders were now routed from Blasowitz by the second battalion of the 13th Light. In fact the *jaeger* and the Austrian horse gunners needed no prompting to abandon the place without more ado, for they saw that Vandamme's powerful French column was deploying on the Staré Vinohrady. On the way back the *jaeger* were badly mauled by the second battalion of the 51st Line, which had meanwhile worked around to the north of the village. Worse still, the French established a battery on the Staré Vinohrady and opened a destructive fire along the length of the Austrian cavalry. Hohen-lohe tried to rid himself of the nuisance by bringing up the regi-ments of Kaiser and Nassau to support the Lothringen Regiment. The three units now moved threateningly on the Staré Vinohrady, but they became entangled in the vineyards and were halted by enemy fire.

Meanwhile Bagration had committed his force along the axis of the highway. His three regiments of line infantry extended across the road, with regiments of dragoons, hussars and cossacks swarming on their front and flanks. On the more distant flanks the 5th *Jaeger* were pushed ahead to Siwitz, while the 6th *Jaeger* occupied Krug to the south of the highway.

> 'The terrain on either side of the Olmütz highway was advanta-geous to the enemy (the French), in that the plateau, on which Prince Bagration's corps stood, descended in a broad and gentle slope towards the Leschner Inn (on the Bosenitzer stream), which prevented the movements of the enemy from being discovered from the front of this corps. From the Santon, however, the enemy could make out the smallest motions of the Russians.'[44]

Marching to encounter Bagration, the young conscripts of Lannes' corps came under a cross fire of artillery which mowed down 400 of their number in a matter of minutes. Lannes took up the artillery duel by unmasking fifteen guns of his own. The Russians came off the worse, for their numerous unicorns were outranged by the French long guns, and all their pieces had to be dragged around by main force, whereas Lannes kept his horse teams well forward and moved his artillery about in a sprightly fashion.

Bagration now put in a powerful attack against Lannes' left wing and the vital Santon mound. Two battalions of the 5th *Jaeger* descended on the scattered French pickets among the woods and vineyards in the direction of Welatitz:

> 'The outposts were overthrown in short order, and only the artillery fire from the enemy left wing prevented the fugitives from being totally wiped out by the cossacks and the Mariupol Hussars, which came hastening up. *Jaeger* and cossacks pressed into Bosenitz itself . . . and surprised a mob of marauders, some of whom were brought back prisoner, and the rest cut down on the spot.'[45]

This impudent attack put at stake the honour of the 17th Light, which Napoleon had commissioned to hold this ground to the utmost. The second battalion accordingly descended from the Santon, and turned the Russians out of Bosenitz about as quickly as they had entered.

Towards noon Lannes was in a position to undertake a general offensive. South of the highway, Caffarelli's division advanced to exploit the success at Blasowitz (see p. 127). General Ulanius put up what resistance he could with the 6th *Jaeger* and detachments of the Tver Dragoons and Pavlograd Hussars, but he was swept in turn from Krug and Holubitz.

The 30th and 17th line regiments could now be sent to the left to support Suchet's division, which was pitted against Bagration's main force of infantry north of the highway. The rival infantry were reasonably well matched at about 5,000 each, but to begin with the French cavalry faced odds of more than two to one.

Every now and then Kellermann's light cavalry or Walther's dragoons would come scampering back from one of their encounters, and try to escape through the gaps in the French infantry. Fortunately for them the counter-attacks of the allied horse were badly co-ordinated. Ermolov complained that 'our cavalry, like the rest of our forces, acted largely on its own account, without any attempt at mutual support. And thus from one wing to another our forces came into action by detachments, and one after another they were put into disorder, overthrown and chased off the field.'[46] The ground in front of the 34th Line was littered with dead and wounded Russian horsemen.

However, the Russian infantry stood firm in compact masses, and the Russian musketry and canister put the French to one of their severest tests in the whole battle. Suchet reported:

> 'Drawn up in lines, our infantry withstood the canister fire with total composure, filling up the files as soon as they had been struck down. The Emperor's order was carried out to the letter (*see p. 83*), and for perhaps the first time in this war, most of the wounded made their way to the dressing stations unaided.'[47]

The sorely-tried 34th Line suffered the further ordeal of seeing General Valhubert fall in front of them, struck down by a shot which shattered his thigh. He refused to have himself carried away: 'I can die just as well here; if one man falls, it doesn't mean we have to lose six.'[48]

It is impossible to reconstruct a wholly convincing sequence of events from the bald statements of Bagration, and the detailed but improbable reports of French victories. What is fairly clear is that the French push along the highway threatened to sever Bagration altogether from the main army to the south. On the far northern flank, the light cavalry of Treilhard and Milhaud chased the 5th *Jaeger* and a swarm of cossacks from the valley of Siwitz. In the centre, the efforts of Kellermann's light cavalry and Walther's dragoons were now backed by the heavyweights of d'Hautpoul's division of cuirassiers. A final cavalry action began on the heights north-east of Posorsitz. General Sébastiani was wounded in the midst of his brigade of dragoons, but the encounter ended with the Russian horse falling back to the valley of Kowalowitz.

The cuirassiers were now free to turn their attention to the right flank of Bagration's infantry. The Russians held the horse at bay with platoon fire, but Suchet meanwhile brought up the superior force of his infantry brigades, and once the impotent cuirassiers were out of the way he drove the Russians from the field in increasing disorder. The exhausted Pavlograd Hussars sought to cover the retreat, and they suffered heavily in the process.

As the French won ground so they began to come across the personal effects which the Russians had deposited before the battle.

> 'We entered into possession of 10,000 [*sic*] knapsacks, which were drawn up in line. The booty was immense at first sight, but all we got were 10,000 little black boxes of two-leaved reliquaries, with the image of St. Nicholas [*sic*] bearing the infant Christ above the waters, and 10,000 pieces of black bread, made of straw and bran rather than barley and wheat. Such were their simple and pious possessions.'[49]

Suchet claims that this final attack killed 2,000 Russians and captured sixteen of their guns.

Bagration established some of his more battleworthy forces in a blocking position on high ground near Welleschowitz, and began to array the rest on the heights of Raussnitz—the cavalry in the first line and the severely-depleted infantry to the rear. He had already abandoned the important fork near the Posorsitz post-house, and was now in danger of being driven up the Olmütz road and clear away from the main army to the south. Providence now decreed that the Austrian Major Frierenberger should arrive on the scene with a train of twelve cannon:

> 'these guns had been sent to the army from Olmütz, and they reached Raussnitz at the moment when fugitives came pouring back to confirm the frightful news of the various disasters experienced by the army. The commander pushed his train along the Brünn highway, and, although he had no real covering force, he positioned the battery . . . on the most advantageous site on the already-mentioned high ground to the right of Welleschowitz. The army he faced was a victorious one. It had deployed at the

Posorsitz post house, and was now in full advance, shooting with its powerful artillery against whatever Russian troops and batteries came into view. The Austrian battery now opened up in its turn against the main battery of the French and their leading troops. The Austrians shot with such extraordinary skill that they compelled the enemy to pull back their batteries in a matter of minutes. Some of the hostile pieces were silenced altogether, and the advance of the whole French left wing was held back. This success was doubly important: it freed Prince Bagration's corps from the pursuit of the enemy, who were now in greatly superior force, and at the same time it denied the French all possibility of executing an attack down the road to Hungary.'[50]

Bagration was now free to rejoin the main army. He had done more than had been expected of him in Weyrother's plan, far more in fact than was conceded by historians until the patient researcher Michel de Lombarès (1947) revealed how much Napoleon's plan of battle demanded an almost unresisted sweep across the northernmost flank of the field.

The march of events had left a knot of Russian cavalry stranded to the south of the highway. This was the brigade of General-Adjutant Uvarov, consisting of the Kharkov and Chernigov Dragoons, the Elisabetgrad Hussars and Lieutenant-Colonel Ermolov's battery of horse artillery. Bagration on the right was falling back, the Austrian cuirassiers had disappeared somewhere over to the left, and powerful masses of French infantry and artillery were bearing down in a threatening fashion before them. After the battle, Uvarov penned a glowing report of his accomplishment in bringing his command back over the Raussnitz stream, and then standing firm under heavy pressure on the heights on the eastern side, thereby enabling the army to make good its escape.[51] Ermolov paints the episode in rather different colours:

'The losses were greatly increased when our forces crowded against an extremely boggy stream (the Raussnitz stream), which could be passed only by a few bridges. Our fugitive cavalry tried to get across by wading, and many of the men and horses were drowned. I was abandoned by the regiment to which I was attached, but I planted my battery in the hope of holding off the enemy, who were pursuing our horse. I extricated one gun from the press of our own cavalry, but we were able to get off only a few rounds before the enemy captured the piece. My men were cut down in the process and I myself was taken prisoner. General-Adjutant Uvarov's division, standing at the bridges, now had the time to appreciate that it had been fleeing from only a small force of the French, and that the main enemy force was still positioned on the heights, not having ventured into the valley. Our pursuers were put to flight and destroyed. So it was that I was freed from my brief captivity, when a dangerously short distance from the French lines. I rejoined the remnants of my shattered battery, and found the division milling about in disorder at the foot of the little hill where the tsar was standing . . . hardly anyone remained of his retinue. His features were lined with deep sorrow, and his eyes were full of tears.'[52]

It is probably convenient to sum up the course of the battle so far:

1. In the south the main allied striking force was still stuck fast on the line of the lower Goldbach.
2. The divisions of Saint-Hilaire and Vandamme had established themselves in the centre on the Pratzen plateau, after their unexpected encounter with the laggardly fourth column of the allies.
3. In their lonely battle to the north, Bagration and Liechtenstein had monopolized the attention of Lannes' V Corps, but were now in retreat.

The Russian Imperial Guard was the last allied formation which had still to be committed to the fight. If its intervention did not bring about the decisive moment of the day (this honour probably belongs to the action on the Pratzeberg) it certainly provided the battle with its most dramatic episode, threatening as it did the French hold on the Pratzen heights, and precipitating by its failure the ruin of the allied army.

Towards the middle of the morning the Grand Duke Constantine Pavlovich was leading the 10,000-odd men of the Russian Imperial Guard in the direction of the high ground south-east of Blasowitz. He had the Preobrazhensky and Semenovsky regiments in his first line, the Izmailovsky Regiment and the battalion of Guard *Jaeger* in the second line, and the cavalry in a rearward line and a reserve.

Constantine was immaculate in a white uniform and black helmet, as befitted a brother of the Tsar. It was galling for a man of his high birth and violent temperament to know so little of what was going on. Towards Blasowitz there were some troops and a battery of artillery, which he took to be part of Liechtenstein's force. He was disabused when the guns opened fire and tore away a file of the Preobrazhensky Regiment. Constantine sent forward his *jaeger* to occupy the place. A battalion of the Semenovsky Regiment followed in their tracks as reinforcements, but the Russians were soon forced to abandon the position as untenable (see p. 127). At about the same time word came from Alexander begging Constantine to send some help to the Pratzen. Colonel Khrapovitsky marched thither with a battalion of the Izmailovsky Regiment, and arrived in time to be caught up in the rout of the fourth column.

All of this brought home to Constantine the fact that the Guard represented the only allied force on the right centre of the field, and that he was now in the forefront of the battle. No further orders came his way, but the detailed Austrian account tells us that he decided that he must recoil to his left rear and establish contact with the beaten fourth column *behind* the Raussnitz stream. Towards half past eleven he accordingly began his march. He covered his right flank and rear by leaving Captain Zocchi with a battery of Austrian reserve artillery on a height above the upper Raussnitz stream, and throwing out the *jaeger* in a screen facing Blasowitz.

Constantine's move afforded welcome relief to the three Austrian cuirassier regiments of Lieutenant-General Hohenlohe (see p. 127), which slipped around the rear of the column and made for Krzenowitz. The further progress of the Guard was however, threatened by the advance of Vandamme's division over the Staré Vinohrady, and Constantine was forced to send the Semenovsky and Preobrazhensky regiments and the *jaeger* to occupy the eastward prolongation of the feature. The Guard cavalry was brought up on either flank, and the grateful Hohenlohe did a kind of about turn, placing the cuirassier regiments of Lothringen and Kaiser on the right rear, and the cuirassier regiment of Nassau on the left towards Zbeischow.

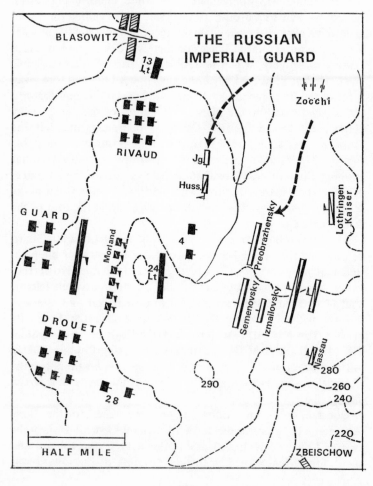

The Guard's show of force was fundamentally a defensive ploy, designed to hold back the French 'so that it could then peel away its front bit by bit and file away through Krzenowitz'.[53] However, a violent fire of musketry broke out on both sides, and on the right flank the *jaeger* battalion and the Guard Hussars found themselves hotly engaged against compact lines of French infantry which were advancing through the vineyards on the northern slopes of the Staré Vinohrady. These hostile forces comprised the left-hand brigade of Vandamme's division (4th and 28th Line and 24th Light). Against his original intention, Constantine was forced to respond by launching a full-scale attack on the Staré Vinohrady.

The Preobrazhensky and Semenovsky Regiments advanced steadily up the slope, then covered the last 300 paces at the run. Though breathless and greatly weakened by musketry, the Russians broke the first line at bayonet point, and were checked in front of the second line only by a terrible artillery fire. Now the finest cavalry of the Russian army arrived to take up the quarrel, led by the 1,000 men of the Guard Cuirassiers, and spurred on by Constantine's cry: 'For God, the Tsar and Russia!'

At this moment Vandamme was sitting on an overturned cart, having his wounds attended. He was unsure of the identity of the approaching column, and sent Major Auguste Bigarré of the 4th Line to investigate at closer range. At the edge of the plateau Bigarré could see a mass of glittering cavalry advancing towards him at a smart trot. He galloped back to the first battalion of the 4th and ordered it to form square to meet the shock. However, the Russians cunningly deployed at long musket range and unmasked six light pieces, which lashed the compact formation of the 4th with canister. Vandamme sent the 24th Light to lend assistance, but he was anticipated by Constantine, who launched two of his regiments against the isolated battalion.

'This first charge failed to penetrate the square, being received by a discharge of musketry at point-blank range. Before we managed to reload, however, a third Russian regiment carried out a fresh charge, sweeping over the square and back again, and cutting down more than 200 men of the regiment. It was in this *mêlée* that a Russian officer seized the battalion eagle from the hands of

Sergeant-Major Saint-Cyr, who relinquished this trophy only after he had received a dozen wounds on his head and arms. Two of his comrades had carried the eagle before him, and both had been killed—one by the Russian canister, and one by a pistol shot.'[54]

Thus the allies gained their one trophy of the battle.

Perhaps hoping to learn from the experiences of the 4th, the companion regiment, the 24th Light, now deployed into line. However, this strung-out formation left it exposed to the great mass of the Guard cavalry, which this time pushed straight on and rode over the regiment.

Riding from his first standpoint on the Zuran hill, Napoleon arrived on the Staré Vinohrady in time to see a cloud of infantry pouring towards him in disorder. ' "What on earth is that?" said Napoleon. "Your Majesty", cried Marshal Berthier, "what a splendid crowd of prisoners they are bringing back for you!" '[55] However, it soon became evident that the troops were fleeing Frenchmen, and that they were repeatedly looking over their shoulders—an indication that hostile cavalry could not be far behind. Such was the force of habit that when the troops streamed past Napoleon they panted out feeble cries of *Vive l'Empereur!* Even Napoleon had to smile at the incongruity of the scene.

The job of plugging the breach fell upon Bessières, as commander of the recently-arrived French Imperial Guard. He sent Colonel Morland hastening forward with two squadrons of the *chasseurs à cheval*, supported on his right by General Ordener and three battalions of *grenadiers à cheval*, and Prince Borghese with a further squadron of the *chasseurs*. Colonel Doguereau's pieces of horse artillery bounced forward to join in the fight.

The moustachioed giants of the Semenovsky Regiment fought back with musketry and battalion guns, and bayoneted a French officer who pushed his way into their ranks. At the same time, their brothers of the Preobrazhensky Regiment took a heavy toll of the French cavalry which tried to attack them in the vineyards north of the Staré Vinohrady.

The French were still engaged in this profitless activity when the remaining regiments of the Russian Imperial Guard were committed to the action, namely the *Chevalier Garde* and the Guard

Cossacks. The Russians attacked from three sides, and the fourth and fifth squadrons of the *Chevalier Garde* hewed with notable effect into the flank of the French cavalry which was engaged with the Semenovsky Regiment.

Napoleon and Bessières now fed the fresh second-line regiments of the Guard cavalry into the action. The stocky General Rapp, the Emperor's senior aide-de-camp, scouted ahead with one squadron of Mamelukes and two squadrons of *chasseurs*. While still out of cannon range he could see the extent of the disaster:

'The cavalry was in the midst of our squares, and was cutting down our soldiers. A little to the rear we could see the masses of infantry and cavalry which formed the enemy reserve. The Russians broke contact and rushed against me, while four pieces of their horse artillery came up at the gallop and unlimbered. I advanced in good order, with brave Colonel Morland on my left, and General Dallemagne to my right. I told my men: "Over there you can see our brothers and friends being trodden underfoot. Avenge our comrades! Avenge our standards!" We threw ourselves on the artillery and took it, and in the same onslaught we overthrew the enemy cavalry, which awaited us at the halt. It fled in disorder, and we all rode over the wreckage of our broken squares.'[56]

The tactics of the Mamelukes proved to be murderously effective. Being 'wonderful horsemen, they could make their mounts do exactly what they wanted. They could sever a head with a single blow of their curved sabres, and with their sharp-edged stirrups they cut into the soldiers' backs.'[57] A Frenchman points out that the Russian infantry made the mistake of levelling their bayonets against the horses' chests. The animals were infuriated by the goading and lashed out with their hooves, breaking into the ranks. 'We would have been beaten, if the Russians had instead aimed their bayonets at the horses' heads, as we did at the Battle of the Pyramids (1798). When he is pricked in the head the horse rears up, unseating his rider.'[58]

However, the *chasseurs* fared rather badly against the huge Russian cavalrymen, who were fighting like maniacs, and Napoleon was forced to send in a squadron of the *grenadiers à cheval*. One of the grenadiers of the foot Guard describes how these 'black horsemen' swept past 'like lightning and crashed into the enemy. For a quarter of an hour there was a frightful *mêlée*, and fifteen minutes seemed like a century. We could see nothing through the smoke and dust, and we were afraid that our comrades were going to be cut up. We therefore advanced slowly behind them, knowing that if they were beaten it would be our turn next.'[59]

To the right General Drouet was bringing up the leading division of Bernadotte's I Corps. Drouet had been marching at Soult's request to reinforce Saint-Hilaire, but he was diverted to the centre at the direct order of Napoleon. The division was moving by columns of half battalion, and at one juncture the Russian cavalry impudently rushed through the intervals and attacked the *chasseurs*, who were rallying to the rear. Drouet greeted the horsemen with blasts of musketry on their return journey, and toppled a good many from their saddles.

The infantry of the Russian Guard was unable to open fire for fear of hitting their own horsemen, and amidst scenes of bitter hand-to-hand fighting, the cavalry was finally pushed towards the Littawa valley. The defeat of the *Chevalier Garde* was particularly horrible:

'This regiment was composed of the most brilliant young men of the Russian nobility, who liked to boast of their superiority over the French. This circumstance became known to our men, who were therefore determined to get their own back, and especially the *grenadiers à cheval*, who skewered them with their enormous swords and cried out: "Here's something for the St. Petersburg ladies to cry about!" '[60]

Marshal Bernadotte afterwards claimed the credit for Drouet's move, but his only major contribution to the events of the day was to halt his corps on the heights above Krzenowitz. Thus the remains of the Russian Imperial Guard were able to file away to safety through the village, covered by the three regiments of Austrian cuirassiers.

Rapp and another of the aides-de-camp had already presented their reports to the emperor:

5. One of the massive barns at Sokolnitz Castle.

6. The charge of the Mamelukes of the French Imperial Guard.

17. The last act: The French advance towards the Satschan Pond while the allie

lumns stream over the ice. Augezd is on the left and Satschan on the centre right.

18. The legend of the ponds—the allies plunge to their destruction beneath frowning cliffs.

19. Francis and Napoleon meet at the Spálény Mill.

'The return journey proved to be even more dangerous than the attack, for our route was under heavy howitzer fire. A *chasseur* of the Guard, who was returning wounded . . . disappeared with his horse when a shell exploded in the animal's belly. Their flesh was blown away, leaving nothing but the shattered bones of the two victims.'[61]

Rapp reached the Staré Vinohrady at the gallop, looking very warlike with his fiery gaze and bloody, dented sabre. Napoleon was standing on horseback on the beaten ground of the summit, with Bessières at his side, and his aides Ségur, Caulaincourt, Lebrun and Thiard standing respectfully to the rear. 'Rapp . . . declared in a loud voice, "Sir, I allowed myself to make off with your *chasseurs*; we have overthrown and crushed the Russian Guard, and taken its artillery!" "Very good, I saw it", replied the emperor, "but I notice you are wounded." Rapp answered, "It's nothing, sir, just a scratch!" '[62]

Morland had been fatally wounded in the action, but the man responsible, Prince Repnin of the fourth squadron of the *Chevalier Garde*, was now presented to Napoleon as a captive. Napoleon's Egyptian servant, Roustam, was clutching another trophy, in the shape of a Russian standard:

'This individual . . . was known in the Guard for his courage and ferocity. During the charge he set off in pursuit of Grand Duke Constantine, who got rid of him only by firing his pistol, which badly wounded his horse. Roustam was upset that the only thing he had to offer the emperor was a standard. He presented the object to Napoleon, announcing in his strange jargon, "Ah! If me catch Constantine, me cut off head, and me bring to emperor!" . . . Napoleon was furious and replied, "Be silent, you ghastly savage!" '[63]

Everything confirmed the extent of the victory. All sorts of horrible sights presented themselves to Napoleon's gaze as he rode over the scenes of combat on the Pratzen:

'The location of that terrible shock was marked by a whole rank of Alexander's young and unfortunate *Chevalier Garde*, who had been struck down from in front and were now stretched out on the ground'[64] '... Everywhere on this vast battlefield the earth was covered with Russian bodies, and whole companies were heaped in bloody piles along their original alignments. Among the great quantity of green-coated corpses were to be seen a number of blue uniforms, but so few that the French themselves were taken aback.'[65]

At this moment a young artillery officer called Apraksin was brought before the Emperor by one of the *chasseurs*: 'he struggled, wept, and twisted his hands in despair, crying out, "I've lost my battery! I've been shamed in front of the whole world! I want to die!" Napoleon spoke consolingly to him. "Be calm, young man! There is no disgrace in being beaten by the French." '[66]

VI THE DESTRUCTION OF THE ALLIED LEFT WING

By his obstinate fight Bagration had prevented the left wing of the *Grande Armée* from fulfilling its mission of turning the right flank and rear of the Russo-Austrian host. In the centre, however, the litter of corpses and wreckage on the Pratzen testified to the defeat of the allied fourth column and the Russian Imperial Guard. Napoleon now made a decisive intervention in the course of the battle. Since the grand sweep from the far left was no longer feasible, he opted for a kind of 'little solution', which nevertheless implied the destruction of more than one third of the allied army. His available striking force would now wheel to the right on the conquered Pratzen, and sweep south against the rear of the three enemy columns still battling on the lower Goldbach. The main responsiblity for the blow rested on the IV Corps, and Saint-Hilaire and Vandamme hurriedly conferred over the details.

The deadly attack began to take shape after two in the afternoon. Saint-Hilaire's division, supported by the centre brigade (46th and 57th Line) of Vandamme's division, peeled off to the right and descended the slopes in the direction of Sokolnitz. The remainder of Vandamme's force marched straight for the wall-like southern edge of the Pratzen plateau, overlooking the allied path

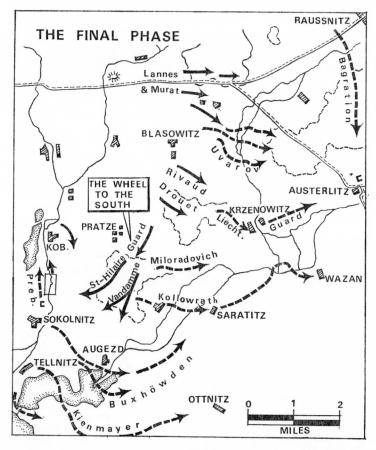

THE FINAL PHASE

RAUSSNITZ

Bagration

Lannes
& Murat

BLASOWITZ

Uvarov

AUSTERLITZ

Rivaud

Drouet

THE WHEEL
TO THE
SOUTH

KRZENOWITZ

Liecht.   Guard

PRATZE

KOB.

St-Hilaire   Guard

Miloradovich

WAZAN

Preb.

Vandamme

Kollowrath

SARATITZ

SOKOLNITZ

AUGEZD

TELLNITZ

Buxhöwden

OTTNITZ

0   1   2

Kienmayer

MILES

of escape. Levasseur's brigade of Legrand's division now emerged
from the area of Kobelnitz and swung into line with Saint-
Hilaire's right, while Legrand in person brought up the 26th Light
and 3rd Line to prolong Saint-Hilaire's left. The dragoon division
of Boyé followed close behind Vandamme, and one of Oudinot's
grenadier brigades came up in the rear. Thus the French force on
the Pratzen consisted of two spearheads—the divisions of Saint-
Hilaire and Vandamme—and powerful mixed supports and
reserves. In the rear Napoleon and the Guard were moving up
from the Staré Vinohrady.

141

Throughout these developments, Friant's division of Davout's III Corps had been clinging stubbornly on to the southern and western exits of Sokolnitz, where they kept the Russian second and third columns tightly bottled up. It so happened that Friant launched a general counter-attack just when the French forces on the Pratzen were poised to fall on the enemy from behind.

To lend the necessary weight to his attack Friant withdrew the 33rd Line from his extreme left and used it to lead the assault against the western salient of the village. The long-suffering 48th Line simultaneously gained ground at the southern edge of Sokolnitz, while the French *tirailleurs* swarmed through the little gardens and began to infiltrate the castle complex.

> 'The main street of Sokolnitz was very wide, and four or five hundred paces long. This extensive area was entirely covered with the dead and wounded of both sides. The corpses were heaped up on one another, and it was almost impossible to ride across the tangle of weapons and broken human bodies.'[67]

Nothing could have been less welcome to Prebyshevsky and Langeron than the news that further enemy forces were descending from the Pratzen against their rear. The bulk of Saint-Hilaire's division bore straight down on the low brick wall and the massed greenery of the Sokolnitz pheasantry, but General Thiébault with the 36th Line executed a circuit to the south and joined Friant's division for the attack on the castle. On Saint-Hilaire's right, Levasseur's brigade was making for the meadows which extended between the pheasantry and Kobelnitz.

The giant pincer movement had the effect of severing the Russians around Sokolnitz into three parts:

1. Langeron and part of his column (the 8th *Jaeger* and the regiment of Viborg) escaped to the south.
2. Another force (the Perm Musketeers of the second column, together with part of the 7th *Jaeger* from the third column) was driven north-westwards clear away from the rest of the army. In the process some of the Russians were crushed against enclosure walls, while others defended themselves like madmen in the castle and its massive farm buildings. Thiébault describes how

'The avenues, the stables, the barns, the outhouses and the parent manor — all acted as little forts for the Russians, who were putting up a desperate fight. In this great slaughter the Russians had to be beaten down man by man. I saw individuals defending themselves as confidently as if they had been in the midst of their battalions. I noticed others, ready to collapse from multiple wounds, loading their muskets as coolly as on the drill square.'[68]

The survivors staged another stand on the higher ground behind the castle, and a party of dedicated gunners caught the 36th Line with a final blast at a range of fifty paces. A score of the French were blown away, and Thiébault himself took a canister ball in his right shoulder.

3. The last clump of Russian forces at Sokolnitz comprised the Galicia and Butyrsk Regiments, which had been fighting in the area of the pheasantry, together with the reserve which had been standing in the open ground to the east, namely part of the regiment of Narva, and the heavily-depleted regiments of Azov and Podolia. Prebyshevsky was present in person, accompanied by Major-Generals Strik and Selekhov. Prebyshevsky was aware that he was cut off to the south, but he could discover so little about the course of the battle elsewhere that he conceived the idea of breaking out to the north, hoping to find the fourth column at its objective of Kobelnitz. He did not know that it was two or more miles away, retiring in disorder to the east.

On the way to this supposed refuge, Prebyshevsky's command was assailed on the right flank by the brigades of Morand and Levasseur, in the rear by the 36th Line, and on the left flank by part of Oudinot's grenadiers. The Russians lost men at every step as they fled along the pheasantry walls, and in the fading light the rest were overhauled on the hard-frozen ice of the upper Kobelnitz pond. Volleys of musketry and canister were sweeping in, and the generals and officers could no longer keep the men in any kind of order. As Prebyshevsky later reported to Alexander,

'We had endured the most intense fire for eight hours . . . One of my subordinate commanders had been killed, another wounded, and the rest were reduced to confusion by the vicious salvoes of canister which came in from three sides. We ran out of cartridges, and we had no hope of support. With all of this we fought on against the enemy to the limit of our strength, according to the loyalty we owe to Your Imperial Highness.'[69]

In these dire moments a number of NCOs and men had the presence of mind to tear the colours from the staffs and hide them beneath their uniforms.

General Lochet and a battalion of the 36th Line pushed their way towards Prebyshevsky with the ambition of taking him prisoner. They had only a short distance to go when Colonel Franceschi hurled himself in the way with a knot of the 8th Hussars. Lochet gave vent to an agonized cry of *Merde!* while the enterprising hussar pointed his sabre at Prebyshevsky and ordered him to tell his men to lay down their arms. Thus 'four thousand infantry surrendered without more ado to a handful of hussars'.[70]

The aide-de-camp Lejeune was riding with a fellow officer and a score of dragoons to report the successes to Napoleon. On the way they crossed the débris of a Russian column. 'One of their generals, dressed very simply, tried to bar our way with a few troops. We pushed straight at them. I pierced the general's arm with my sword, while Sopranzy seized the bridle of his horse, and we dragged him into our ranks.'[71] The captive turned out to be no less than Lieutenant-General Wimpfen, who had been separated from the main body of the reserve, and was trying to escape with a party of men from the Narva Regiment.

All the rest of the allied forces were cut off to the south of Sokolnitz, in other words the remnant of Langeron's column, and the commands of Dokhturov and Kienmayer. The escape of these formations was threatened not only by Davout and Saint-Hilaire, pressing respectively from the west and north, but much more dangerously by Vandamme's infantry and Boyé's Third Division of Dragoons, which threatened to cut across the rear.

Napoleon meanwhile had ridden over the Pratzen, and joined Vandamme and Soult at the Chapel of St Anthony, some way down the southern slopes. At his feet lay the village of Augezd, which offered the only apparent path of retreat for the allies as they flooded from the right to left across the darkening plain.

Beyond them again stretched two level and white expanses – the legendary frozen ponds of Satschan and Menitz.

There was a maddening delay in reaching out for Augezd, for Vandamme's troops were arriving in dribs and drabs, and a mass of Russian artillery (variously estimated at between twenty-four and fifty pieces) was pelting the hillside with shot and shell. For a time the French were unable to reply. They had about twenty-five guns of their own trundling across the plateau, but the train was slow to arrive. On the way it was actually threatened by a party of the Austrian Erzherzog Johann Dragoons. These men had led the advance of the allied fourth column, and they had been roaming the Pratzen ever since.[72]

At last a lone battalion of the 28th Line led the way by descending to the east of Augezd and cutting the road to Hostieradek. Finally the main force (the 24th Light, the 4th Line and the remaining battalion of the 28th) swept past on either side of the chapel and descended on Augezd 'like a torrent'.[73] It was taken after a short but violent exchange of fire, and Colonel Sulima of the 8th *Jaeger* was counted among the many prisoners. The Russian gunners stood by their pieces to the last, and fired at such short range that some of the French troops were scorched by the flames. One of Vandamme's battalions arrived at the spot scarcely 150 men strong. Ségur exclaimed in astonishment, and Vandamme rejoined, 'Yes, I know. But you can't make omelettes without breaking eggs!'[74]

The allies were threatened with imminent annihilation. Up till now a small detachment at Tellnitz had screened the retreat of the bulk of the first column and the survivors of the second. This gallant force stood under the immediate direction of Dokhturov and Kienmayer, and comprised the cossacks and the Austrian left-wing cavalry, together with a handful of Croatian, Székler and Russian infantry. With characteristic professionalism the two generals began to pull their forces out of the village and prosecute a fighting retreat around to the south and east, trusting to the firmness of the frozen ponds.

'Lieutenant-General Kienmayer's Austrian cavalry took the lead. The infantry followed in a single column, breaking off in succession from the left wing, and retired along the narrow spur between the village of Tellnitz and the Satschan pond. They maintained good order, even though they were under a continuous fire of musketry and canister. Tellnitz was now abandoned, and Prince Moritz Liechtenstein formed the rearguard with a force of Austrian cavalry, together with some cossacks which had joined them. The O'Reilly *Chevaulégers* Regiment drove back the pursuing enemy cavalry, and kept up an accurate fire with its battery of horse artillery, silencing several French guns; the regiment's action covered the retreat of the infantry, which was carried out in good order over the Satschan pond and so on towards Neudorf.'[75]

Kienmayer took precautions against any disturbance from the direction of Augezd: three battalions remained for a time in Satschan village, and the Hessen–Homburg Hussars were arrayed on the low ridge between that place and Ottnitz.

The ineffectual French cavalry was in fact the entire Third Dragoon Division of General Boyé. Napoleon had naturally expected great things when the dragoons first descended the slopes towards Tellnitz, and he was furious to see them fall tamely back to the Pratzen. 'This put the emperor in an evil temper. He caught sight of a general staff officer who had accompanied the division. "Go back there", said the emperor, "and tell the general in command from me that he's no bloody good!" A fine mission for an aide-de-camp!'[76] General Gardane was nominated to take over the division, and the spare staff officers dashed off to take part in a new attack. From the Russian sources it seems that in the dust and murk the French ran into a deadly fire from fifteen or twenty pieces of Russian artillery, commanded by Colonel Sievers. In turn the French unmasked six cannon of the Guard Horse Artillery, which delivered a salvo at point-blank range into the Austrian cavalry.

The effort was much too late. The 'Tellnitz' detachment was making good its escape, and all the French had to show were some Austrian prisoners. Captain Thiard indentified 'some of the O'Reilly *Chevaulégers*, which was one of the finest regiments of the Austrian army, together with some Croats, with their blue pants and felt shakoes. I interrogated them upon the emperor's order. When I asked the name of their commanding general they

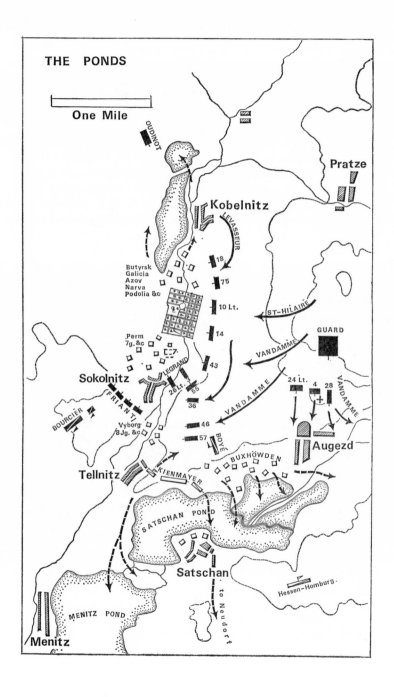

THE PONDS

One Mile

OUDINOT

Pratze

Kobelnitz

LEVASSEUR

18

Butyrsk
Galicia
Azov
Narva
Podolia &c

75

10 Lt.

ST-HILAIRE

GUARD

14

VANDAMME

Perm
7g. &c

43

Sokolnitz

LEGRAND

26Lt. 3

55

FRIANT

36

VANDAMME

24 Lt.

4 28

VANDAMME

BOURCIER

Vyborg
8 Jg. &c

46

57

BOYÉ

Augezd

Tellnitz

KIENMAYER

BUXHÖWDEN

SATSCHAN POND

Satschan

Hessen-Homburg

to Neudorf

MENITZ POND

Menitz

replied "Kienmayer". Soldiers recall a name as easily as this when they consider themselves fortunate to come under the man's command.'[77]

The remainder of the left wing ended the day with much less dignity. Buxhöwden was in possession of an order from Kutuzov to extricate his command from the Goldbach. He at first intended to break through to the fourth column along the north bank of the Littawa. This ambition was frustrated by the progress of the French at Augezd, and Buxhöwden decided instead to cut across to the south bank by way of the rickety bridge just below that place. He and his staff were among the first to make the passage, as we might expect. The guns and caissons that followed broke the bridge and stuck fast, leaving almost the whole of the Russian artillery stranded on the north bank, ready to be picked up by the French. The Russian infantry accordingly made straight across the Satschan pond, the surface of which was blackened by the thousands of fleeing men.

Some of the artillery of the 'Tellnitz' detachment was meanwhile filing over the causeway between the two ponds. Unfortunately,

'the mass of men retreating over the ice of the Satschan pond attracted the fire of the enemy cannon on the chapel hill at Augezd* to the area of the causeway. An ammunition cart was struck by a howitzer shell on the causeway and blew up, provoking a jam among the pieces which were travelling up behind. Some of the artillery of the column was therefore left on the field, and part of the infantry now made their retreat across the ice of the Menitz pond; luckily the surface was frozen so hard that it bore the weight of the mass of troops without breaking. Just two men and a few of the horses fell through. Their bodies were found afterwards, when the ponds were drained.'[78]

During these minutes 'the sun sank beneath the dense clouds along the horizon, and at the same moment the snow began to fall, like the curtain descending in a theatre at the close of the last act'.[79]

Such was the slender basis for the extraordinary claim of the

---

* The guns in question were probably nearer than this.

30th Bulletin of the *Grande Armée,* that 20,000 Russian troops flung themselves into the ponds and drowned. On the French side the Comte de Comeau was close enough to see what had happened. He points out that most of the Russians actually swarmed around the edges, and that 'even if a few platoons paddled in the water, it was not deep enough to have drowned them'.[80]

If the Russians were merely rounded up by the French, rather than engulfed in the icy water, their losses still ran into many thousands. Napoleon now rode down to the plain in the company of Marshals Soult and Bessières. At his approach the officers and soldiers raised their headgear on their swords and bayonets and shouted with joy. 'No longer could you recognize the conscripts among the old warriors. The experiences of this day had been worth ten years' campaigning.'[81]

Fire ceased all over the field by half past four, and in the first hours of darkness the weary French settled down on the same ground which had been held by the allies just before the battle. On the northern flank Bagration had fallen back to a blocking position at Raussnitz (see p. 130). Then, hearing that the army was to retire on Hungary, he abandoned the Olmütz highway and the baggage and cut across to Austerlitz. He arrived there late in the evening, and met Miloradovich with the Russian survivors of the fourth column. Liechtenstein's cavalry and the Russian Imperial Guard were also kept well in hand, and they spent the night in front of Austerlitz on the heights overlooking the Raussnitz stream.

Less happily, Kutuzov, Kollowrath and Kamensky were forced to by-pass Austerlitz to the south and make their retreat by way of Wazan and Hodiegitz. Buxhöwden trailed up behind them along the south bank of the Littawa. He had just two battalions with him—a sorry remnant of the 33,000 or so troops he had commanded in the morning. Prince Czartoryski saw him come in. 'The poor general had lost his hat, and his uniform was in disarray. As soon as he caught sight of me he cried out, "I've been abandoned! I've been sacrificed!"' '[82]

The village of Czeitsch on the road to Hungary was designated the rallying point for the whole army. The losses of the Russians appeared even greater than they really were, for so many troops were scattered in the darkness across the countryside. The artillery and knapsacks had been abandoned on the field, and the wretched country tracks dissolved in the sleet and icy rain which had been falling since half past three in the afternoon. 'So much confusion and disorder never attended any retreat.'[83]

Nothing was known of the whereabouts of Alexander, though it was reported that he had been wounded in the battle and rushed away in a coach. The defeated Tsar was first detected by Major Toll, who was astonished to see Alexander riding back across country, accompanied only by the surgeon Wylie and the head groom Iene. Toll followed at some distance, anxious for the Tsar's safety, but not wishing to intrude on his privacy. After a while Alexander dismounted and sat on the damp ground beneath a tree, where he covered his face with a cloth and burst into tears. His two companions stood by in embarrassment, but Toll came quietly to his side and spoke some consoling words. Alexander got to his feet, silently embraced Toll, and rode on to Hodiegitz. The village was full of wounded soldiers, but in all the confusion a captain of horse was able to find Kutuzov and bring him to Alexander for a hurried conference. There were no carriages to be had, and so Alexander had to plunge on through the darkness and rain. Seven miles travelling brought him to Urchitz, where he collapsed on a pile of straw in a peasant's hut, and was lulled to an exhausted sleep by camomile and opium and a draught of wine.

After their stupendous victory the French were content to take their rest. Not only had Bagration broken free of Lannes, but he had been allowed to pass unmolested across the nose of Bernadotte's I Corps, poised on the slopes above the Raussnitz stream. Murat received no fresh orders from Napoleon, and so the bulk of the French cavalry remained inactive on the left centre of the army.

The French troops made themselves as comfortable as they could on the hideous field. Many of them were far too excited to sleep, and spent the night re-living the events of the day, and debating what name the victory would bear. There was general admiration for the uncomplaining Russian wounded, who clung together in heaps, or dragged themselves to the warmth of the French fires.

Napoleon, Berthier and Soult rode slowly from the region of the ponds to the highway in the north, picking their way with difficulty over the wreckage of the battlefield:

'It was night already, and Napoleon ordered his entire suite to remain silent, so that we could hear the cries of the wounded. Whenever he heard one of these unfortunates he went to his side, dismounted, and made him drink a glass of brandy from the store which followed him everywhere . . . the squadron of his escort spent the whole night stripping the Russian corpses of their great-coats, with which to cover the wounded.'[84]

Towards ten Napoleon reached the little Posorsitz post house, which the Russians had used as a dressing station. The Emperor and his senior officers crowded into the two rooms and dried their steaming clothes at a huge fire, while the nearest soldiers brought in food from their bivouacs. Napoleon began to dictate a proclamation, but in his weariness he chose to complete the address on the following day:

'Soldiers, I am pleased with you! You have, on this day of Austerlitz, justified everything that I had expected of your boldness, and you have honoured your eagles with an immortal glory. In less than four hours an army of 100,000 men [sic], commanded by the emperors of Russia and Austria, has been cut down or scattered. Such enemy as escaped your bayonets have been drowned in the lakes . . . Soldiers, when I have accomplished everything that is necessary for the happiness and prosperity of your land, I shall lead you back to France. There you will be the objects of my most tender care. My people will greet you with joy, and it will be enough for you to say "I was at the Battle of Austerlitz", and they will reply "There stands a hero!" '

VII EXPLOITATION AND ARMISTICE

Emperor Francis (for so long absent from our story) met Alexander and Kutuzov at Czeitsch at noon on 3 December to debate what was to happen next. The choices were severely limited, for the French were across the road to Olmütz, and Alexander was bent on extricating his troops by the one remaining route, which lay through Hungary. Reinforcements were close at hand (Merveldt with 4,000 Austrian survivors from Mariazell and other parts arrived on the 4th, and General Essen with 12,000 fresh Russians appeared two days later), but nothing could redeem a campaign that was already considered lost. The Russian army was to continue its retreat to Hungary by way of the bridge over the March at Göding, while Francis addressed himself to Napoleon and gained what terms he could for the Austrians. Francis later wrote bitterly about the way he had been abandoned by his ally: 'After the battle Tsar Alexander strongly urged the total withdrawal of the Russians, if he did not actually demand it. This step deprived us of a support that we badly needed, now that we had to bargain for peace.'[85]

The gallant Prince Johann Liechtenstein had already betaken himself to the Posorsitz post house before dawn on 3 December, and arranged a preliminary interview between the two emperors. Napoleon was gratified by this development, but in every other respect he found that the day after the battle was wasted. The cavalry swept the countryside to see where the allies were going, but 'reconnaissances of this kind, so vital in warfare, were always performed badly by our army'.[86] Murat sent back a mistaken report that the Russians had returned to the Olmütz road, and V Corps and the main body of the cavalry were accordingly dispatched to the north-east. Napoleon in person rode to Austerlitz, and it was only here that he learnt that the allies were actually recoiling in the direction of Hungary.

Napoleon spent the night in the sumptuous surroundings of the Kaunitz Castle at Austerlitz, and on the morning of the 4th he donned a clean shirt (his first in eight days) and the dark green and white severity of the uniform of the *chasseurs* of the Guard. Between nine and ten the Emperor set off at a gallop for the appointed meeting place with the Austrians, a mill where the road to Hungary crossed the Spálény stream. The party soon reached the brow of the hill above the stream. 'On our side the top of the valley was crowned by the French Imperial Guard, with fluttering colours and scarlet plumes, arrayed as if for a review. Away in the distance, the remains of the Austrians faced us on the opposite side.'[87] Napoleon sent Ségur down to make the necessary arrangements. The Emperor was determined to obtain a quick peace on harsh terms, and it suited his purpose to make the circumstances of the interview as 'military' as possible. The sappers of the Guard lit a large fire in a small grassy amphitheatre, and the *chasseurs* fixed a plank to a tree trunk to serve as a seat. The ground began to thaw in the warmth of the flames, which persuaded the party to lay a track of straw between the road and the fire. Napoleon smiled at the preparations and remarked, 'That's quite enough for my purposes. But remember it took six months to arrange the ceremonial for the meeting of Francis I and Charles V!'[88]

At two in the afternoon a light carriage came into sight, accompanied by one squadron each of Austrian hussars and uhlans. 'At the same moment the drummers of the Guard beat *aux champs*, while the trumpeters sounded the march. The sight was magnificent.'[89] The Austrian cavalry halted 200 paces away, but the carriage continued and stopped on the road opposite the fire.

Napoleon went to the door and made as if to embrace his fellow Emperor, but he was checked by the Austrian's abstracted air. However, Francis proceeded to warm the atmosphere with a few genial words, and the French could begin without embarrassment to take in the appearance of their guest and his sole companion, Prince Liechtenstein.

> 'Francis was scarcely thirty-six years old, but he was enveloped in an enormous buttoned-up greatcoat, he wore a three-corned hat at the back of his head, and he was carrying a stick. From his outfit you might have thought he was an invalid. Prince Johann was a small figure, in his white coat and uniform, girdled by a golden sash, but his bearing was as assured and lively as the manner of Francis was solemn. Somewhat younger than Francis, he wore his hat in the fashion of the French military men, namely fore-and-aft.'[90]

The Emperors' conversation lasted for less than an hour. Their attendants could hear little of what they were saying, but bursts of laughter carried across the air, and towards the end Francis appeared oddly cheerful. They parted after a final hug. In effect

Francis had gained an armistice for himself and his allies, to take effect on the following day.

The allied army meanwhile continued to evade the pursuit in a galling manner. Soult and his IV Corps were notably slow in getting under way on the 4th, and the chase was spearheaded by Davout's III Corps, which had been reinforced by the fresh division of Gudin. By three in the afternoon the light cavalry at Davout's head came to within striking distance of the retreating allies, as they crossed the vital bridge over the March at Göding. At this juncture Merveldt sent a colonel to tell the French that an armistice was already in force, in virtue of the meeting then taking place between Napoleon and Francis. Davout was justifiably suspicious, but the allies backed up their argument by producing a letter from Kutuzov and a pencilled message of confirmation from Alexander himself. Thus wily old monarchical Europe won the last trick in the game of fraud and bluff which began at the Vienna bridge three weeks before.

General Savary reached Göding with the news of the Spálény agreement on the night of the 4th, and he was astonished to find that hostilities had already ceased. Alexander received him on the far bank at the castle of Hollitsch. He gave his assent to the terms which had been agreed between Francis and Napoleon, and promised to leave the Austrian dominions at all reasonable speed.

On the way back to Austerlitz, Savary had to wait at the Göding bridge while the Russian army continued across the March, on their way to Russia and ultimately to wars anew. 'No more than 26,000 men passed by, all arms included. Most of them had lost their knapsacks, and a great many were wounded, but they marched bravely in their ranks.'[91]

Almost forgotten, the field of Austerlitz festered slowly in the icy air. A wandering Moravian found

'thousands of corpses stretched out on the ground one by one or in heaps. The expression on their faces was frightful to see. Hands, feet, dismembered bodies and trunks were scattered about. At one place a cripple stretched out his bloody hand and cried for help. Elsewhere we saw a soldier who had sunk up to his waist in mud and was half frozen.'[92]

Six weeks more and

'traces of the slaughter were still to be seen all over the field. The many freshly-turned piles of earth betrayed the sites of the graves. Everywhere we saw shattered weapons, and torn clothing which was spurned by even the poorest of the peasants. We repeatedly had to hasten past spots where inadequately buried bodies of horses had been worked over by the ravens and crows, and were spreading an intolerable stench. Worse still, you could see the severed limbs of dead or maimed soldiers, together with half-eaten skulls, bones and ribs.'[93]

CHAPTER 9

NAPOLEON'S GREATEST VICTORY

I THE PRICE

IT is generally reckoned that the total allied losses in casualties, prisoners and missing amounted to some 27,000 men, or in other terms the very high proportion of about one-third of their effectives. A few details can be supplied. The Russian lists (excluding all the Guard save the Guard Cuirassiers) give us totals of 19,886 for the cavalry and infantry, and 3,616 for the artillery.[1] Altogether eighteen convoys of prisoners passed through Brünn, comprising 9,767 Russians and 1,686 Austrians.[2] There remains a difference of 13,735 between the reported number of Russian prisoners and the total Russian loss. After making allowance for the prisoners from the Guard, it is reasonable to suppose that a high proportion of the remainder must have been killed. The passage of time has lent the events at Austerlitz a certain glamour and excitement, but it is sobering to reflect that so many men who were alive at the beginning of the day were dispatched to literally 'God knows what'.

From the total loss of about 3,500 Austrians we must deduct the 1,686 prisoners. The balance of about 1,800 casualties and missing leads us to suppose that the 33rd Bulletin of the *Grande Armée* was not far wrong in putting the Austrian dead at 600. It is likely that the Austrians sustained most of their losses at the peak of the combat, whereas the Russians lost proportionately more at the end of the day, when they were reduced to mobs.

Many of the men were probably rendered *hors de combat* by wounds, and then bayoneted to death by the French.

The resourceful Kienmayer managed to bring off his guns. Otherwise the first, second and third columns lost their entire artillery, which helped to bring the loss in allied ordnance to 180 pieces. Between forty-five and fifty colours and standards also fell to the French.

The losses of the *Grande Armée* were extraordinarily light, amounting to a total of some 8,000. This figure is made up of 1,305 killed, 573 captured, and about 6,940 wounded. Certain divisions bore more than their fair share of the butcher's bill, as might have been expected from the course of the fighting: Friant lost 1,900 men, Saint-Hilaire 1,776 and Vandamme 1,456. However, the regimental lists show some curious discrepancies. The 24th Light suffered no less than 126 killed and 364 wounded, whereas the 4th Line, which was ridden over just as comprehensively by the cavalry of the Russian Guard, managed to escape with just eighteen dead.

II THE JUDGMENTS

After the shattering blow of Austerlitz, Major Toll could not at first understand how it was that Weyrother's precise and apparently well-considered plan had precipitated such a disaster.[3] What had gone wrong? Most of the survivors seem to have hit fairly soon upon the fundamental reason, namely that their army was not up to the tactical outflanking move which had been demanded of it.[4]

Informed contemporaries were able to enter into a number of particulars. Sir Arthur Paget believed that the day was lost once the allies found the French established on the crossings of the lower Goldbach. 'This unexpected reception led to the most fatal consequences.'[5] Langeron rightly dismissed the theory that Napoleon must have discovered the allied plans: 'It is just possible, but, whatever people say, he could easily have deduced them from his military experience and his *coup d'oeil*.'[6] He could see almost the whole extent of the allied bivouac fires, which was enough to tell him that the main concentration was directed against his right. The same points are made by the Austrian, General Stutterheim, who was with Kienmayer's detachment. He adds that the allied columns were spaced so far apart that they gave one another very little support.[7] (See also pp. 104–5).

Napoleon was reluctant to accuse the allied commanders of *fautes principales*, and from what we know now of the course of the battle it seems that only the drunken, immobile and selfish Buxhöwden emerges as a true incompetent. This did not prevent the Russian authorities from instituting a witch hunt among their generals. The toadies around the Tsar actually blamed Kutuzov for failing to use his weight of experience and knowledge to deter the allies from accepting combat in the first place.

Kutuzov himself drew Alexander's attention to the failings in the centre:

'As Your Imperial Highness could see for yourself, the fourth column was chiefly responsible for the advantage the enemy gained on that day. Two battalions of the Novgorod Musketeers ran away without offering the slightest resistance, which spread fear and panic among the whole column.

'Moreover the third column was gravely at fault. Its commander (Prebyshevsky) took no precautions and got his men stuck in the village of Kobelnitz, giving the enemy the chance to outflank the column and capture most of the troops.'[8]

On returning from captivity in France, Prebyshevsky was cleared of the charge of cowardice, but convicted of a number of basic misjudgments:

'The commander of this column did not fulfil the disposition with the accuracy that duty demands. He did not take suitable measures for the retreat along the road to Hungary. He failed to maintain constant communication with the other columns and his reserves. He divided his forces, and was consequently unable to support the various detachments, or supply the troops with cartridges. Nor could he unite with his reserves, or retire on the locality which had been designated. Finally he had to retreat with a mob of troops in a direction which was precisely the opposite to the one stipulated.

He arrived in complete disorder, he was surrounded by the enemy, and he surrendered.'[9]

Buxhöwden was cunning enough to direct attention from himself by getting in a number of blows against Langeron. Disclaiming all responsibility for the doings of the second column (even though it stood under his command), he criticized Langeron for getting stuck in the village of Sokolnitz, instead of passing the valley between there and Tellnitz. Here Buxhöwden attached some blame to the Austrian guides, but he arraigned Langeron on the further charge of sending Kamensky to be destroyed, whereas he should have combined with the first column and counter-attacked the Pratzen with united forces. He had made the acquaintance of Langeron as a staff officer, and in this capacity had found him brave and intelligent, 'but there is a distinction to be made between a staff officer and a general'. By this standard Langeron was lacking in experience and presence of mind.[10]

One day Langeron received a letter from Count Lieven:

'The events of 2 December were particularly unfortunate for the column under Your Excellency's command, and His Majesty is dissatisfied at the way in which this column was led. In order to spare your feelings he has therefore ordered me to tell you that you have permission to request your resignation.'[11]

Langeron had to prove himself on many battlefields before Alexander finally relented and restored him to grace.

On the day of battle, according to one account, 'Grand Duke Constantine gave way to a wild and ill-considered enthusiasm, which degenerated into a savage fury. He spoiled everything by his violence.'[12] However, Kutuzov was courtier enough to praise the Grand Duke for the achievement of his Imperial Guard, which took the only trophy of the day, and finally retired in such good order. Defeat was inevitable, he wrote, in view of the superior numbers of the enemy, 'but in the midst of all this misfortune the prudence of Your Highness stood out all the more clearly'.[13]

There was no concealing the misconduct of the Novgorod Musketeers. Against this must be set the example of heroes like

Kamensky's troops, who pitted themselves against an entire division, or the devotion of certain NCOs and men of the Perm, Azov, Narva and Galicia Regiments, who salvaged and concealed their colours at the end of the day. The soldiers in general gave a good account of themselves, and Napoleon himself maintained that 'the Russian army which fought at Austerlitz would not have lost the battle of Borodino'.[14]

Some of the Russian regimental officers acquitted themselves well, but far too many of the others simply fled the field. Buxhöwden cites the disgraceful conduct of one of the Podolia Musketeers, two of the Elisabetgrad Hussars and two more of the Old Ingermanland Musketeers, five of the Arkhangelgorod Musketeers, and no less than nine of Constantine's regiment of uhlans. The commander of the baggage train had seen many more sneaking among his carts.

However, nobody in the Russian army was more embarrassed than Colonel Kudryatsev of the 3rd Artillery Regiment, who gave up his battery for lost early in the fight. Ten days later, after a saga of untold effort, the *Feuerwerker* fourth-class Dmitry Kabatsky turned up out of the blue with two of the pieces in question, as well as an ammunition cart and seventeen gunners.

Few things are more surprising in the battle than the performance of the homeless Austrians, who rarely fought less than well, and sometimes brilliantly. If two dozen Austrian generals were purged after the war, this was the result of the disgraceful episodes on the Danube rather than on account of any failings at Austerlitz. In 1807 Mack was deprived of his commission and honours, and sentenced to two years' detention in a fortress.

For the French, the outcome of the battle represented the fulfilment and justification of everything for which the *Grande Armée* had been training during the previous three years. Stutterheim conceded that 'the French infantry manœuvred with coolness and precision, fought with courage, and executed its bold movements with admirable concert'.[15] The cavalry overcame the very best that the Russians could put in the field, and when Napoleon heard of the damage inflicted by his artillery he remarked 'these successes afford me great pleasure. I have not forgotten that it was in this corps that I began my military career.'[16]

What of Napoleon's personal contribution? There is something very impressive about his light but firm control of affairs, as exemplified by his 'right turn' on the Pratzen towards the end of the day. In contrast the allies were left without wit or resource, once the situation ceased to correspond with the calculations of the Weyrother plan.

However the most telling comment on Napoleon's management of the battle arose during Savary's candlelight conversation with Alexander in the castle of Hollitsch, early on the morning of 5 December. The Tsar congratulated Savary on the victory, but emphasized that the French apparently had superior forces all over the field. Savary had to point out that the French were actually inferior:

> 'What really happened was that we moved about a good deal, and that individual divisions fought successive actions in different parts of the field. This is what multiplied our forces throughout the day, and this is what the art of war is all about. This was Napoleon's fortieth battle, and he never goes wrong on that point.'[17]

The infantry of the French Imperial Guard had nothing to do save occupy the ground which had been won by other forces, and the grenadiers were reduced to weeping with frustration. Out of the eighteen battalions of Bernadotte's I Corps only about half ever fired their muskets, while Oudinot's grenadiers appeared only in time to help to round up Prebyshevsky's shattered remnants at Kobelnitz. Altogether Napoleon calculated that he could have won his battle with 25,000 fewer troops than he actually had.

The burden which rested on IV Corps was all the heavier, and General Thiébault complained that the division of Saint-Hilaire got feeble support during its epic battles on the Pratzen, and precious little recognition afterwards.

In all other respects Napoleon was generosity itself. He disbursed 2,000,000 francs among the higher officers. He awarded large pensions to the widows of that day, and he extended his Imperial protection to the orphans it created. One of the dead heroes, Colonel Morland, had his memory preserved in corporeal form. He was pickled in a cask of brandy and brought to Paris.

Fifteen years later the cask broke up, and the colonel was found to be in a good state of repair, though his moustaches now extended down to his waist. The body passed into the possession of a savant, who kept it with him as a curiosity: 'Pursue the paths of glory, and you end up by getting yourself killed so that some big-headed naturalist can place you in his study, half way between a rhinoceros horn and a stuffed crocodile.'[18]

III AUSTERLITZ IN HISTORY

As battles go, Austerlitz could not be considered an exceptionally large engagement, whether in terms of the combatants involved or the size of the slaughter, 'but it is the consequences of the action of 2 December, 1805; it is the epoch when it decided the fate of the war; it is the *moment* in which it was fought, which makes it worthy of attention, and which will assign it a marked place in history.'[19]

While Kutuzov led his army back to Russia, clutching a gracious letter of farewell from Emperor Francis, Napoleon made his way to Vienna and carried through an important rearrangement of the map of Europe. He first of all bought off the Prussians, by allowing them to grab the electorate of Hanover, and he then made individual deals with his faithful clients in Germany. All of this boded ill for Austria, which was forced to accept Napoleon's terms in the Treaty of Pressburg of 27 December, 1805. Writing to Alexander, Francis could not conceal from him that the treaty 'turned out to be a capitulation before an enemy who pressed home his advantages to the full. The sorry state of affairs has forced me to abandon part of my provinces, so that I may preserve the rest.'[20]

Venetia, Friuli, Dalmatia and Istria were made over to the parvenu kingdom of Italy. More painfully still, the Tyrol and Vorarlberg were relinquished to the detested Bavarians, and a scattering of enclaves in Germany were ceded to Württemberg and Baden. The duke of Baden was now elevated to grand duke, and the electors of Württemberg and Bavaria were proclaimed kings, no less. Austria lost 2,500,000 subjects, and forfeited the predominant position she had enjoyed in Germany for centuries.

On 11 January, 1806, the French relinquished the keys of Vienna to the municipality, and over the following weeks their troops filed out of the truncated remnants of Austria.

The grand strategic diversions which had been planned by the allies came to very little. The Russian and Swedish forces which landed in north Germany did not venture very far inland. The Anglo-Russian expedition to Italy actually landed in Naples and made some little progress, but it turned back immediately on hearing news of the disaster at Austerlitz.

The later history of the Napoleonic empire may be regarded as a decline from the peak that had been attained at Austerlitz in 1805. Napoleon beat the Prussians in 1806, and the Russians again in 1807, but already the cohesion of the *Grande Armée* was being weakened by indiscipline and wastage, and the incorporation of non-French elements.

Inevitably the defeated Austrians, Russians and Prussians set out to reform their armies on modern lines. No less importantly, the peoples began to discover a sense of nationhood in the face of Napoleon's naked drive for personal and family power. In 1809 the Austrians embarked on a new war in a wave of national enthusiasm. Napoleon was once more victorious, but this time it cost him two battles and 50,000 men to get across the Danube near Vienna. In the following year one of his officials returned to the city, and found that everything had changed: 'They were preparing for revenge not just among the Imperial family, the cabinet, the grandees and the army, but—what was much more dangerous—in the hearts of the people as well.'[21]

The troops of a great anti-Napoleonic coalition entered Paris in 1814, and for a second and final time in the next year. On the first occasion it was suggested to Alexander that he should blow up the Pont d'Austerlitz. He replied: 'There is no need for us to touch the bridge. It will be enough if history records that the Russian army once marched across it.'[22]

On the allied side, the analysis of the great battle got off to a bad start when Alexander asked Kutuzov to draw up two relations, one for the Tsar's own eye, and another one specially designed to counter the French publicity. Kutuzov knowingly misrepresented the allied losses at under 12,000, and claimed that the guns had to be left behind because of the mistakes of the Austrian guides.

Fortunately the Austrian, General Stutterheim, lost no time in getting down to work, and within a couple of years his published account reached a wide European audience. The book is remarkably objective, considering that it was composed so soon after the event.

The first full-length Russian examination of the campaign and battle was drawn up by Lieutenant-General Mikhailovsky-Danilevsky (1844). The work is convincing enough in its own terms, but as the veteran staff officer Toll pointed out, the action unfolded much less neatly than you would have concluded from this account.

The later non-French historians are somewhat disappointing, at least to a student of the battle. Military pundits treated the campaign as a text-book example of the art of war, and were content to base their accounts almost entirely on the French sources. The more scholarly works of Austrian and modern Soviet historians concentrate largely on the events which preceded the battle—the Austrians (Angeli, Krauss, Egger, etc) seeking to explain episodes like the capitulation of Ulm and the loss of the Vienna bridge, while the Russians stress the importance of Kutuzov's 'march manœuvre' from Braunau to Moravia.

The French look back on Austerlitz with a nostalgic glow, composed of the vivid recollections of veterans and the superb canvasses of contemporary artists like Bacler d'Albe and Gérard. Until the present century, however, any study of the battle distinctly lacked subtlety. The day was thought to have been virtually won the moment that the IV Corps mounted the Pratzen, as Napoleon would have liked people to believe. The picture is lent dramatic interest by the intervention of the Russian Guard, and the battle closes with the mass-drowning of the allied army on the ponds.

The myth of the ponds was dispelled by the researches of the Moravian archivist Janetschek in 1898, and not long afterwards Commandant J. Colin carried out the herculean task of establishing the detailed sequences of events from the point of view of the

Grande Armée (1906–07). Among other things Colin showed that the battle for the Pratzen was far more bitter and protracted than had previously been supposed.

The better-known of the more recent French offerings may be variously categorized as hagiographies or entertainments. However, in 1947 M. de Lombarès performed a service of fundamental importance when he uncovered the development of Napoleon's intentions concerning the battle, and demonstrated how little the action as fought corresponded with the Emperor's plans. Napoleon's powers of improvisation now became all the more important: the IV Corps advance on the Pratzen, which was planned as just one element of a much wider sweep, therefore became the chief instrument of victory.

Leaving the historians to argue among themselves, we must conclude by taking into consideration the great novel *War and Peace*. People have found in it not only the most vivid of all accounts of Napoleonic campaigns, but a true and timeless representation of what warfare signifies to the individuals who are caught up in it. Tolstoy's classic was completed in 1896, and it has since been presented as film (King Vidor, first shown 1956; Sergei Bondarchuk, 1968), television serial (John Davies, BBC 1972–73), and opera (Prokofiev, 1944 with later revisions).

In the novel the treatment of the campaign of 1805 takes up Book II and much of Book III. Tolstoy conveys a great deal of information in a variety of ways—straightforward historical narrative, snatches of dialogue, sharply-observed set scenes, and above all the experiences of two of the major characters of the book, namely the twenty-year-old hussar, Count Nicholai Rostov, who is painfully anxious to make a good impression, and the staff officer, Prince Andrei Bolkonsky, whom we encounter in detached and supercilious mood.

The scene opens on the Russian army as it gathers at Braunau, and we follow the two protagonists through Kutuzov's retreat and the action at Schöngrabern. Tolstoy presents a magnificent re-creation of the parade of the allied army outside Olmütz, and shows how an impressionable soul like Nicholai could be caught up in the surge of worship for the young Tsar Alexander.

The description of the battle of 2 December begins on an

ominously low note, with the allied columns shuffling over the Pratzen in the mist. Delays and rumours spread a feeling of uncertainty among the troops, and we attend the famous exchange between Kutuzov and the impatient Alexander.

Suddenly the French surge on to the Pratzen and Andrei is involved in the collapse of Miloradovich's command. He seizes a fallen colour, and leads a battalion a little way in a counter-attack before he is felled by some unspecified blow to the head. Regaining consciousness some hours later, he hears Napoleon in person exclaiming at the sight of his motionless body. Andrei has rediscovered some of the meaning of life, and he moans and stirs, lest he should remain on the field as a dead hero. Napoleon at once orders him to be carried away and tended.

Nicholai has meanwhile managed to get himself attached to Bagration as an aide. The general is unwilling to take the responsibility of attacking without orders (here Tolstoy does Bagration a severe injustice), and he sends Nicholai to gain the authorization from Kutuzov. This narrative device allows Nicholai to traverse a cross-section of the field. On the way south he is nearly caught up with the fleeing uhlans of Constantine's regiment, and again with the charge of the cavalry of the Guard. He passes the Guard infantry during a lull in the action, but arrives behind Pratze village to find the French on the heights and the fourth column in disarray. There is no sign of Kutuzov, and the demi-god Alexander is espied in a pale and haggard state, making his way from the field.

With these episodes Tolstoy brings the campaign of 1805 to a close. What were his sources? Much that lends animation to the story—the vignettes of military life, the sensations of men in action—comes from his own experience of war in the Caucasus and the Crimea. Mikhailovsky-Danilevsky's history has obviously supplied the narrative backbone, as well as details like the dialogue between Alexander and Kutuzov on the Pratzen. The celebrated council of war in the presence of the dozing Kutuzov is drawn straight from Langeron's account, while the distant sight of the French torchlight procession comes probably from Ermolov. Toll's recollections furnish the particulars of Alexander's dejected retreat from the battle. Quite possibly Toll provided Tolstoy with further inspiration, this time of a more philosophical kind, when he spoke of the divorce between Mikhailovsky-Danilevsky's well-ordered account of the fourth column's battle on the Pratzen, and what he knew of the muddled actuality.[23]

IV THE BATTLEFIELD TODAY

The scenes of the great events have changed little since 1805. The city of Brünn (Brno) is the obvious base for any expedition to the field of Austerlitz, and pilgrims could do worse than put up at the Grand Hotel, situated opposite the railway and bus stations. Travelling by car, just under six miles of the Olmütz road (E 7) brings you to the bare ridge of the Zuran hill, where a little road leads to the site of Napoleon's first command post on the summit three hundred yards to the right. Here stands a stone cube surmounted by a map in bronze relief (1931), which usefully sets out the arrangement of the armies at seven on the morning of the battle. From this viewpoint the field seems a good deal more extensive, and the various 'heights' considerably lower that you would expect from some sources. The Santon appears as a distant green bump to the left centre, and to the right you can make out the low and ragged profile of the Pratzeberg, with its distinctive monument.

To reach the Santon you return to the main road and continue to the turning on the left to Bosenitz (Tvařozná). At the western entrance to the village a track crosses a little valley and strikes up through the young trees which annoyingly obliterate the outline of the hill. Only on reaching the top is it possible to appreciate the strength of the position. The climb from Bosenitz has been steep enough, but the slope to the north-east is more acute still, and the northern side is frankly precipitous. The little white chapel on the grassy summit was built in 1832 to take the place of the original, which was demolished by the French before the action.

In case you are in need of refreshment, you can retrace your steps along the E 7 and take the first turning on the left after the Zuran, which leads south by way of Bellowitz (Bedřichovice) to Schlapanitz. The little road winds through the orchards which carpet the floor of the narrow valley of the upper Goldbach, and we can appreciate how well the French reserves must have been screened from the view of observers to the east. Schlapanitz (Slapanice) has grown considerably towards the west and south, but the core of the old village is largely intact, and the former monastery school which housed Bernadotte's headquarters has now been turned into a small museum. Pilsener, pork and dumplings are available in the plain but genial restaurant in the small square just before the fork of the roads to Slatina and Kobelnitz.

With morale restored you can take the road from Schlapanitz to Puntowitz (Ponětovice) across the forming-up area of Saint-Hilaire and Vandamme. From here we notice just how low the Pratzen saddle appears from the valley. The little road to Pratze (Prace) follows the axis of Saint-Hilaire's advance. The course of the fighting at Pratze is difficult to follow on the ground, and the devastated church was completely rebuilt in 1810. However, the village makes a good base for exploring the central part of the field. From the north-eastern side a road climbs steadily to the windy ridge of the Staré Vinohrady, that strange feature which seems prominent enough from the valley, but which vanishes almost completely when viewed from the Zuran or the Pratzeberg. The encounter between Alexander and Kutuzov probably took place where the side road to Blasowitz (Blažovice) branches off to the left. To avoid an unduly long trek across arable land, you can most conveniently reach the pimple-like summit of the Staré Vinohrady by following the Blasowitz road for about 400 yards, which leaves you with just over 200 yards across country.

From the top of the Staré Vinohrady the famous horizon of Austerlitz stretches on all sides. Blasowitz and the area of Liechtenstein's cavalry action lie to the north, and the saddle to the Pratzeberg extends to the south over the ground of the fourth column's battle. The rival forces in this part of the world must have been spread very thinly indeed, and we begin to suspect that our vision of Napoleonic warfare has perhaps been distorted by the crowded little field of Waterloo.

Our next aim is the monument on the Pratzeberg, which from this distance appears to be the offspring of an unsuccessful pyramid and a collapsed bell-tent. The quickest route thither is down to Pratze again and up on the steepish road to the south. At close quarters the monument, or 'Tumulus', appears more hideous still. It was raised in 1912 in the incongruous interests of Pan-Slavism and Peace. The sealed crypt in the base contains the scattered human remains which are still found on the field today, though the greater number of the brave men rest in some twenty-two mass graves. The plain chapel on ground level is devoid of interest save for a curious echo, and for a warrior who reposes in a glass-topped coffin. He does not appear to be in the best of health. A modest single-storey museum (1928) is located to the rear of the Tumulus.

Westwards from the Pratzeberg there is an excellent view over the plain of the lower Goldbach. The green oblong of the Sokolnitz pheasantry is unmistakable. To the north we can make out the roofs of Pratze village, crouching in its hollow, and to the east again the eye follows the site of Kollowrath's action to the brow overlooking the valley of the Littawa. It is not a good idea to attempt to reach the southern slopes above Augezd, for the low straggling wood behind the Tumulus conceals a Soviet military radar station, alive with whirling and nutating aerials.

The road due west from Pratze leads to Kobelnitz (Kobylnice), and thence by a couple of turns carries on in the direction of Maxdorf (Dvorska) and Turas (Tuřany). It is worth travelling as far as the first rise in the road, and looking back towards Kobelnitz over the site of the destruction of Prebyshevsky's column. Here as elsewhere the ponds have been drained, but it is easy enough to retrace their shape by reference to the 190-metre contour line.

The corresponding road south from Kobelnitz soon picks up the low brick wall which encloses the northward extension of the Sokolnitz pheasantry. Nearer to Sokolnitz itself, the site of a French battery has been indicated by five crosses, incised in the wall. All along this stretch the view eastwards to the Pratzen is intact. At the entrance to the village the famous castle turns out to be a sturdy yellow-washed country house, partly restored in the neo-Gothic style. The substantial barns and granaries still extend to the rear, but the rest of Sokolnitz is a tangle of more recent housing and factories, sprawling in an unpleasant fashion in the direction of Augezd (Ujezd). The Goldbach has been reduced to a narrow ditch.

Spirits are raised by the sight of the pleasant church and village centre of Tellnitz. On the south-eastern fringe we find the sheltering bank and the little gardens and vineyards, just as they were described in 1805, when they were swarming with the *tirailleurs* of the 3rd Line. The circuit by way of Satschan (Satčany) and Augezd traverses the area of the Menitz and Satschan ponds. The legend of the mass drownings is certainly false, but there is something undeniably sinister about these level fields of black earth, criss-crossed by power lines, and cringing under the southern slopes of the Pratzeberg.

The road east-north-east from Augezd to Austerlitz follows the Littawa valley. The view to the left is dominated by the rearward slopes of the Pratzen, which are far steeper and more impressive than the corresponding gradients towards the Goldbach. We can only wonder at the risk taken by Napoleon when he abandoned such a commanding feature.

Austerlitz (drearily renamed Slavkov) is notable for the castle, or rather palace, of the Kaunitz family. The pile was built on the grand scale in the eighteenth century, and it offered suitable lodging for Emperor Francis on the night before the battle, and for the victorious Napoleon from 3 December onwards. The ground floor houses a museum of relics, maps and objects of popular art connected with the battle. Immediately outside, the large neo-classical church (1789) bears testimony to the taste of Prince Wenzel Anton von Kaunitz, and its cool atmosphere provides a pleasing foil to the barbaric events of the Napoleonic age.

NOTES

CHAPTER 1 THE THREE EMPERORS

1. *Civilisation*, London 1969, 304
2. Bourienne, VII, 2
3. *Correspondance*, 9166, XI, 167
4. D'Hautpoul, 247
5. Czartoryski, I, 285
6. Ibid, I, 386
7. Rovigo, II, 175–76
8. Czartoryski, I, 262
9. Angeli, *Mittheilungen*, 384
10. Ibid, 422
11. *Kutuzov. Sbornik*, II, 27

CHAPTER 2 THE GRANDE ARMÉE

1. *Mélanges*, I, 243–44
2. Major Coffin, introduction to Stutterheim, 7–8
3. Ségur, II, 339
4. François, 546
5. Brun-Lavaine, quoted in Anon. *Austerlitz Raconté*, 28–29
6. Ibid, 27
7. D'Hautpoul, 286
8. Ibid, 271
9. Bigarré, 161
10. Pion des Loches, 134
11. François, 548
12. Brun-Lavaine, in Anon. *Austerlitz Raconté*, 27
13. Comeau, 205, 214
14. Bigarré, 161
15. Pelleport, I, 203–04
16. Colin, XXVI, 519
17. Levasseur, 31
18. Ibid, 59
19. Bourienne, VII, 10
20. *Correspondance*, 9188, XI, 182
21. Saint-Chamans, 32

CHAPTER 3 THE ARMIES OF OLD EUROPE

1. Angeli, *Zeitschrift* 1877, 424
2. Regele, 147–48
3. Colin, XXVI, 313
4. Angeli, *Zeitschrift* 1877, 461
5. Krauss, 83
6. Muller, 84
7. Angeli, *Zeitschrift* 1877, 429
8. Spoken to E. M. Arndt, and quoted in his *Reisen*, new ed. Vienna 1913, 180
9. Beskrovny, 10
10. Janetschek, 39–40
11. *Kutuzov. Sbornik*, II, 264
12. Wilson, 43–44

13. Russian Gen. Staff, pt. 4, bk. 1,
    sect. 3, vi, n.1
14. Wilson, 4
15. *Kutuzov. Sbornik*, II, 96
16. Russian Gen. Staff, pt. 4, bk. 1,
    sect. 3, iii, 162
17. Ibid, 176
18. Beskrovny, 32
19. Wilson, 33
20. Quoted by Paget 8 Nov., PRO
    FO 7/75

CHAPTER 4 THE RUIN OF THE AUSTRIANS AT ULM

1. Angeli *Mittheilungen*, 378
2. Regele, 152
3. 24 Oct., PRO FO 7/75
4. Pion des Loches, 133
5. Coignet, 164–65
6. Barrès, 33
7. Bigarré, 165
8. *Correspondance*, 9293, XI, 263
9. Comeau, 207
10. Paget 24 Oct., PRO FO 7/75
11. Angeli *Zeitschrift* 1877, 463
12. Paget 1 Nov., PRO FO 7/75
13. *Correspondance*, 9381, XI, 324
14. Ségur, II, 383
15. Krauss, 161
16. Ibid, 477
17. Ségur, II, 397
18. Barrès, 45
19. Raguse, II, 320
20. Ségur, II, 409

CHAPTER 5 KUTUZOV BREAKS FREE

1. To Czartoryski 23 Sept., *Kutuzov.
   Sbornik*, II, 53
2. Orders for the forced march
   23 Sept., Ibid, II, 68
3. To Czartoryski 23 Sept., Ibid,
   II, 53
4. Ibid, II, 68
5. Angeli *Mittheilungen*, 300
6. Ermolov, I, 9
7. Colin, XXIV, 339
8. Rovigo, II, 156
9. Ibid, II, 167
10. Mikhailovsky-Danilevsky, 89
11. Paget 13 Jan. 1806, PRO FO
    7/79
12. Enclosure in Paget's dispatch of
    8 Nov., PRO FO 7/75
13. Jean-Pierre Blaise, in Fairon and
    Heuse, 102
14. Lejeune, I, 29
15. Levasseur, 40
16. Lejeune, I, 31
17. Kutuzov to Alexander 6 Nov.,
    Kutuzov. Sbornik, II, 146
18. Ségur, II, 429
19. Ermolov, I, 13
20. Colin, XXIV, 535
21. Ibid, XXIV, 537
22. Ségur, II, 432
23. Oksman, 70
24. Rapp, 58
25. Angeli *Mittheilungen*, 337
26. Fantin des Odoards, 63
27. Paget 8 Nov., PRO FO 7/75
28. Comeau, 224
29. Thiard, 188
30. *Kutuzov. Sbornik*, II, 352
31. Weyrother's *Tagebuch*, KA FA
    Deutschland 1805 XIII 59
32. 19 Nov., *Kutuzov. Sbornik*, II,
    171
33. To Kutuzov 17 Nov., Ibid, II,
    164
34. Marbot, I, 244
35. Pouget, 69
36. Mikhailovsky-Danilevsky, 131
37. KA *Ausführliche Relation*
38. Ermolov, I, 29

CHAPTER 6 DUEL OF WITS IN MORAVIA

1. Rovigo, II, 188
2. Fantin des Odoards, 68
3. Ibid, 69
4. Levasseur, 58

5. Thiébault, III, 438–39
6. Thiard, 201
7. Thiébault, III, 457
8. Ségur, II, 451
9. Rovigo, II, 199
10. Czartoryski, I, 403
11. Russian Gen. Staff, pt. 2, bk. 1, 179
12. Paget 13 Jan. 1806, PRO FO 7/79
13. Stutterheim, 36
14. Oksman, 81–82
15. Ramsay 25 Nov., PRO FO 7/78
16. Langeron, in Anon. *Austerlitz Raconté*, 147
17. 19 Nov., PRO FO 7/75
18. KA Weyrother's *Tagebuch*
19. Stutterheim, 40
20. Ermolov, I, 30

21. Thiébault, III, 448–49
22. Janetschek, 38–39
23. Ségur, II, 448
24. Rovigo, II, 198–99
25. Thiard, 213
26. Ségur, II, 451–52
27. Lombarès, 65. In the doctored version, which is reproduced in most books, Napoleon talks about the enemy coming to attack his right. The original, stressing the centre, corresponds to the situation as Napoleon saw it on 30 Nov.
28. Comeau, 228
29. Ségur, II, 454
30. Ibid, II, 454–55
31. Thiard, 216

CHAPTER 7   GROUND, FORCES AND PLANS

1. Thiard, 226
2. Ségur, II, 457
3. Ibid, II, 460
4. Rovigo, II, 203
5. Thiard, 219
6. Lejeune, I, 34
7. Or so the 30th Bulletin would have us believe. The accounts of the torchlight procession vary in many particulars. Marbot attributes the initiative to a *chasseur à cheval* of Napoleon's escort, while Bigarré places the incident in the bivouacs of the first grenadier company of the 4th Line. In his very circumstantial relation Thiard moves the whole event back to Napoleon's first tour, immediately after supper
8. Thiébault, III, 452–53
9. KA Weyrother's *Tagebuch*
10. Czartoryski, I, 406
11. Ermolov, I, 32
12. Quoted in Anon. *Austerlitz Raconté*, 126
13. *Disposition* KA FA Deutschland 1805 XII 12
14. Ibid
15. Paget 13 Jan. 1806, PRO FO 7/79
16. Bernhardi-Toll, I, 177
17. Ermolov, I, 33
18. Thiébault, III, 45
19. Rovigo, II, 203–04
20. Barrès, 55–56

CHAPTER 8   'A STORM OF FURY AND BLOODSHED',
2 DECEMBER, 1805

1. Ségur, II, 462
2. Ibid, II, 463
3. Ibid, II, 465
4. Thiébault, III, 457
5. Ibid, III, 458
6. Czartoryski, I, 407
7. Mikhailovsky-Danilevsky, 181–182
8. Ermolov, I, 33–34

9. Pétiet, 28
10. Ségur, II, 466
11. Stutterheim, 100
12. Lejeune, I, 36
13. Fairon and Heuse, 105
14. KA *Ausführliche Relation*
15. Ibid
16. Pouget, 71–72
17. Prebyshevsky to Alexander 11

July, 1806, *Kutuzov. Sbornik*, II, 269

18. Friant 3 Dec., Davout, I, 215
19. Davout to War Ministry, Ibid, I, 20
20. KA *Ausführliche Relation*
21. Colin, XXVI, 531
22. Mikhailovsky-Danilevsky, 184
23. Thiébault, III, 469–70
24. KA *Ausführliche Relation*
25. Thiébault, III, 47–48
26. It is possible that we are dealing here with the reconnaissance of Thiébault and Morand, given some discrepancy between the timings of the various witnesses
27. KA *Ausführliche Relation*
28. Ibid
29. Thiébault, III, 476
30. Ibid, III, 477
31. Colin, XXVI, 529
32. Ibid, XXVII, 381
33. Stutterheim, 106
34. Miloradovich to Kutuzov 3 Dec., *Kutuzov. Sbornik*, II, 231
35. Kutuzov to Alexander 1 March, 1806, Ibid, II, 265
36. Wolzogen, 28
37. Ségur, II, 468
38. Barrès, 56–57
39. Coignet, 472–73
40. KA *Ausführliche Relation*
41. Thiard, 228–29
42. Levasseur, 62
43. Colin, XXVI, 543
44. KA *Ausführliche Relation*
45. Ibid
46. Ermolov, I, 36
47. Colin, XXVI, 545
48. Ibid, XXVI, 545
49. Lejeune, I, 36–37
50. KA *Ausführliche Relation*
51. Uvarov to Kutuzov 7 Dec., *Dokumenty Shtaba M. I. Kutuzova*, 222–23
52. Ermolov, I, 36–37

53. KA *Ausführliche Relation*
54. Bigarré, 176
55. Saint-Chamans, 25–26
56. Rapp, 61
57. Coignet, 473
58. Martin, 54
59. Coignet, 474
60. Marbot, I, 261
61. Lejeune, I, 37–38
62. Ségur, II, 470
63. Marbot, I, 261–62
64. Ségur, II, 471
65. Pétiet, 32
66. Ségur, II, 471
67. Lejeune, I, 38. Lejeune calls the place 'Menitz', which is more than two miles to the south. The context makes it clear that Sokolnitz is intended
68. Thiébault, III, 479–80
69. 11 July, 1806, *Kutuzov. Sbornik*, II, 268
70. Pétiet, 33
71. Lejeune, I, 39
72. KA *Ausführliche Relation*
73. Stutterheim, 121
74. Ségur, II, 474
75. KA *Ausführliche Relation*
76. Saint-Chamans, 27
77. Thiard, 233
78. KA *Ausführliche Relation*
79. Lejeune, I, 41
80. Comeau, 231
81. Pétiet, 37
82. Czartoryski, I, 410
83. Paget 13 Jan. 1806, PRO FO 7/79
84. Rovigo, II, 209
85. Angeli *Mittheilungen*, 360
86. Rovigo, II, 210
87. Ségur, II, 478
88. Ibid, II, 478
89. Thiard, 244
90. Pétiet, 43–44
91. Rovigo, II, 221
92. Janetschek, 138
93. Ibid, 144

CHAPTER 9   NAPOLEON'S GREATEST VICTORY

1. *Kutuzov. Sbornik*, II, 235–36
2. Colin, XXVII, 407–10
3. Bernhardi-Toll, I, 194
4. Wolzogen, 29

5. 3 Dec., PRO FO 7/79
6. Quoted in Anon. *Austerlitz Raconté*, 115
7. Stutterheim, 130–31. See also Ermolov, I, 33
8. Kutuzov's confidential report 13 March, 1806, *Kutuzov. Sbornik*, II, 265
9. Mikhailovsky-Danilevsky, 215
10. To Kutuzov 13 Jan., 1806, *Kutuzov. Sbornik*, II, 262
11. Mikhailovsky-Danilevsky, 214
12. Gentz to Jackson 5 Dec., Weil, 133
13. 8 Dec., *Kutuzov. Sbornik*, II, 228
14. Mikhailovsky-Danilevsky, 216
15. Stutterheim, 132
16. 31st Bulletin, *Correspondance*, 9546, XI, 460
17. Rovigo, II, 219
18. Marbot, I, 265
19. Stutterheim, 15
20. Mikhailovsky-Danilevsky, 244
21. Thiard, 190–91
22. Mikhailovsky-Danilevsky, 246
23. Bernhardi-Toll, I, 184

BIBLIOGRAPHY

a) *Manuscript sources*

Kriegsarchiv (KA) Vienna: *Feldacten* for the northern theatre in 1805, esp. Weyrother's operational *Tagebuch* FA Deutschland 1805 XIII 59, and the detailed account of Austerlitz in FA Deutschland 1805 XI 66¼ *Kurzgefasste Beschreibung der in dem Feldzug 1805 . . . gemachte Bewegung nebst einer Ausführlichen Relation der am 2 ten Dezember, 1805 . . . vorgefallenen Schlacht* (abbreviated for our purposes to *Ausführliche Relation*)

Public Record Office (PRO) London: Reports of the Earl of Harrington, Sir Arthur Paget, and Brigadier-Generals Ramsay and Clinton, Foreign Office Papers (FO) 7/75–79

b) *Printed sources*

Anon. *Austerlitz Raconté par les Témoins de la Bataille des Trois Empereurs,* Geneva 1969

P. C. Alombert and J. Colin *La Campagne de 1805 en Allemagne,* Paris 1902–08. Completed up to mid-November 1805. A massive compilation of narrative and supporting documents

S. Andolenko *Aigles de Napoléon contre Drapeaux du Tsar,* Paris 1969

M. Angeli 'Ulm und Austerlitz' in *Österreichische Militärische Zeitschrift,* Vienna 1877–78, continued in *Mittheilungen des K. K. Kriegs-Archivs,* Vienna 1878

M. Angeli *Erzherzog Carl,* Vienna 1897

General Bagration. Sbornik Dokumentov i Materialov, Moscow 1945

J.-B. Barrès *Souvenirs d'un Officier de la Grande Armée,* Paris 1923. A *vélite* of the Guard in 1805

T. Bernhardi *Denkwürdigkeiten aus dem Leben des Kaiserl. Russ. Generals . . . von Toll,* 4 pts. Leipzig 1865. Compiled from the verbal recollections of a Russian staff officer.

L. G. Beskrovny *Russkaya Armiya i Flot v XIX Veke,* Moscow 1973. Good on Russian military organization

Mémoirs du General Bigarré, Paris undated. He was effective commander of the 4th Line at Austerlitz

Mémoirs de Bourienne, 10 vols. Paris 1829

D. G. Chandler *The Campaigns of Napoleon*, London 1967. Already established as a classic of military history

Les Cahiers du Capitaine Coignet (1799–1815), Paris 1883

J. Colin 'La Campagne de 1805 en Allemagne', in *Revue Historique Rédigée à l'Etat-Major de l'Armée*, XXIX–XXVII, Paris 1906–07. Indispensable for military detail

Baron de Comeau *Souvenirs des Guerres d'Allemagne*, Paris 1900. Many interesting observations from an *émigré* in the Bavarian service, attached to the *Grande Armée* in 1805

O. Criste *Erzherzog Carl*, Vienna 1912

Mémoirs du Prince Adam Czartoryski, 2 vols. Paris 1887

Correspondance du Maréchal Davout, 4 vols. Paris 1885

Marshal Drouet, Comte d'Erlon *Vie Militaire*, Paris 1844

Souvenirs du Lieutenant-Général Comte Matheiu Dumas, 3 vols. Paris 1839

R. Egger *Das Gefecht bei Hollabrunn und Schöngrabern*, Vienna 1975

Zapiski A. P. Ermolova, 2 vols. Moscow 1865–68

V. J. Esposito and J. R. Elting *A Military History and Atlas of the Napoleonic Wars*, London 1964

E. Fairon and H. Heuse *Lettres de Grognards*, Paris 1936

Journal du Général Fantin des Odoards, Paris 1895. A captain in Oudinot's grenadiers in 1805

Journal du Capitaine François, 2 vols. Paris 1903–04. The not-altogether reliable recollections of an artillery officer

A. d'Hautpoul *Souvenirs sur la Révolution, l'Empire et la Restauration*, Paris 1904. A lieutenant of artillery in 1805

C. Janetschek *Die Schlacht bei Austerlitz*, Brünn 1898. Much interesting material, drawn from local accounts

E. P. Karnovich *Tsarevich Konstantin Pavlovich*, St Petersburg 1899

A. Krauss 1805. *Der Feldzug von Ulm*, Vienna 1912

M. I. Kutuzov. Sbornik Dokumentov, 5 vols. Moscow 1950–56

H. Lachouque *Napoléon à Austerlitz*, Paris 1961

Mémoirs du Général Lejeune, 3 vols. Paris 1895

Souvenirs Militaires d'Octave Levasseur, Paris 1914. A lieutenant of horse artillery in 1805

M. Lombarès 'Devant Austerlitz. Sur les Traces de la Pensée de L'Empereur', in *Revue Historique de l'Armée*, III, Paris 1947. The most important of the recent French studies

Souvenirs Militaires du Général Comte de Lorencez, Paris 1902

C. Manceron *Austerlitz*, Paris 1963 and London 1966. Best regarded as a very readable novel, inspired by the events of 1805

Mémoirs du Général Baron de Marbot, 3 vols. Paris 1891

E. Martin *Le Centenaire d'Austerlitz*, Paris 1905. Much useful detail

Lt-Gen Mikhailovsky-Danilevsky *Opisanie Pervoi Voiny Imperatora Aleksandra s Napoleonom v 1805–m Godu*, St Petersburg 1844

P. Muller *L'Espionnage Militaire sous Napoléon 1er*, Paris 1896

Correspondance de Napoléon 1er, 32 vols. Paris 1858–70

R. F. Oer *Der Friede von Pressburg*, Münster 1965. On the diplomatic background

G. V. Oksman 'Marsh-Manevr M. I. Kutuzova v Kampany 1805 G', in *Polkovodets Kutuzov*, ed. L. G. Beskrovny, Moscow 1955

A. Palmer *Alexander I*, London 1974

Souvenirs Militaires et Intimes du Général Vicomte de Pelleport, 2 vols. Paris 1857

A. Pétiet *Souvenirs Militaires de l'Histoire Contemporaine*, Paris 1844

Journal de Marche du Grenadier Pils, Paris 1895

Pion des Loches *Mes Campagnes (1792–1815)*, Paris 1889. A captain on the artillery staff in 1805

Souvenirs de Guerre du Général Baron Pouget, Paris 1895. Colonel of the 26th Light in 1805

Mémoirs de Duc de Raguse (Marmont) de 1792 à 1832, 9 vols. Paris 1857 etc

Mémoirs du Général Rapp, Paris 1823

O. Regele 'Karl Freiherr v. Mack und Johann Ludwig Graf Cobenzl. Ihre Rolle im Kriegsjahr 1805', in *Mittheilungen des Österreichischen Staatsarchivs*, XXI, Vienna 1968. On the Austrian war preparations

H. C. Rogers *Napoleon's Army*, London 1974

Mémoirs du Duc de Rovigo (Savary), 8 vols. Paris 1828

Russian General Staff *Stoletie Voennogo Ministerstva*, St Petersburg 1902–13. Esp. on the work of the staff and codes of tactics

W. Rüstow *Der Krieg von 1805*, Frauenfeld 1853

Mémoirs du Général Comte de Saint-Chamans, Paris 1896. He was on Soult's staff in 1805

K. A. Schimmer *Die Französischen Invasion in Österreich und die Französen in Wien in den Jahren 1805 und 1809*, Vienna 1846

C. R. Schönhals *Der Krieg 1805 in Deutschland*, Vienna 1873

Histoire et Mémoirs. Par le Général Comte de Ségur, 8 vols. Paris 1873

Mémoirs Militaires du Baron Seruzier, Paris 1894. A captain of light artillery in 1805

F. Stein *Geschichte des Russischen Heeres*, Hanover 1885

A. A. Strokov *Istoriya Voennogo Iskusstva*, Moscow 1965

A Detailed Account of the Battle of Austerlitz by the Austrian Major-General, Stutterheim, London 1807. Still the best Austrian printed source

Souvenirs Diplomatiques et Militaires du Général Thiard, Paris 1805. A member of Napoleon's suite in 1805

Mémoirs du Général Baron Thiébault, 3 vols. Paris 1894. The most informative of the French eyewitness accounts

J. Thiry *Ulm, Trafalgar, Austerlitz*, Paris 1962. A useful general survey of the course of 1805. Makes good use of the Bavarian archives

Tranchant de la Verne *Rélation de la Bataille d'Austerlitz*, (1810) Paris 1897

Ed. M.-W. Weil *D'Ulm à Iéna. Correspondance Inédite du Chevalier de Gentz avec Francis James Jackson*, Paris 1921

R. Wilson *Brief Remarks on the Character and Composition of the Russian Army*, London 1810

Memoiren des Königlichen Preussischen Generals der Infanterie Ludwig Freiherrn von Wolzogen, Leipzig 1851

APPENDIX

THE FORCES AT AUSTERLITZ*

A. THE GRANDE ARMÉE (*with nominal establishments*)

Commander-in-Chief & Head of State, EMPEROR NAPOLEON
Chief of Staff, MARSHAL BERTHIER

Imperial Guard, MARSHAL BESSIERES
(5,500 and 24 guns)

Brig. Hulin	Grs. (grenadiers) à Pied
Brig. Soulès	Chasseurs à Pied
Col. Lecchi	Grs. of Royal Italian Guard
Brig. Ordener	Grs. à Cheval
Col. Morland	C. à C. (Chasseurs à Cheval) of Guard
Brig. Savary	Gendarmerie d'Elite
	Guard Mamelukes

I Corps, MARSHAL BERNADOTTE
(13,000 and 24 guns)

Advance guard

27th L.I.R. (Light Inf. Regiment)

1st Div.
Gen. Rivaud de la Raffinière

8th I.R. (Line Inf. Regiment)
45th I.R.
54th I.R.

2nd Div.
Gen. Drouet d'Erlon

94th I.R.
95th I.R.

* Compiled from a variety of sometimes contradictory sources. Neither side had a set order of battle.

III Corps, MARSHAL DAVOUT

2nd Div. (3,800 and 9 guns)
  Gen. Friant
  1st Bde., Brig. Heudelet   108th I.R.
                                Voltigeurs of 15th L.I.R.
  2nd Bde., Brig. Kister   15th L.I.R.
                                33rd I.R.
  3rd Bde., Brig. Lochet   48th I.R.
                                111th I.R.

4th Dr. Div. (2,500 and 3 guns)
  Gen. Bourcier
  Brigs. Laplanche, Sahuc, Verdière
  1st line,   15th Dr. (Dragoon) R.
                                17th Dr.R.
                                27th Dr.R.
  2nd line,   18th Dr.R.
                                19th Dr.R.
  1st Dr.R. was attached independently to III Corps

IV Corps, MARSHAL SOULT
(23,600 and 35 guns)

1st Div.
  Gen. Saint-Hilaire
  Brig. Morand   10th L.I.R.
  Brig. Thiébault   14th I.R.
                                36th I.R.

2nd Div.
  Gen. Vandamme
  Brig. Varé   43rd I.R.
                                55th I.R.
  Brig. Schinner   4th I.R.
                                24th L.I.R.
                                28th I.R.
  Brig. Férey   46th I.R.
                                57th I.R.

3rd Div.
  Gen. Legrand
  Brigs. Merle, Féry   26th L.I.R.
                                3rd I.R.
  Brig. Levasseur   18th I.R.
                                75th I.R.
                                Tirailleurs du Pô
                                Tirailleurs Corses

Light Cav. Div.
  Brig. Margaron   8th Hus.R. (Hussar Regiment)
                                11th C. à C.R.
                                26th C. à C.R.

3rd Dr. Div.
  Brig. Boyé
  Brig. Scalfort   5th Dr.R.
                                8th Dr.R.

                    12th Dr.R.
                    16th Dr.R.
                    21st Dr.R.

              V Corps, MARSHAL LANNES
              (12,700 and 20 guns)

Div. Gen. Caffarelli
  Brigs. Demont, Debilly, Eppler
  1st line,   30th I.R.
                              17th I.R.
                              13th L.I.R.
  2nd line,   51st I.R.
                              61st I.R.

Div. Gen. Suchet
  Brigs. Beker, Valhubert, Claparède
  On Santon,   17th L.I.R.
  1st line,   34th I.R.
                              40th I.R.
  2nd line,   64th I.R.
                              88th I.R.

Light Cav. Div.
  Brig. Treilhard   9th Hus.R.
                              10th Hus.R.
                              13th C. à C.R.
                              21st C. à C.R.

              Gr. Div., GEN. OUDINOT
              (5,700)

Brigs. Mortières, Dupas, Ruffin
Elite bns. of 9th, 13th, 58th, 81st I.R.s, and 2nd, 3rd, 12th, 28th, 31st,
  15th L.I.Rs.

              Cav. Res., MARSHAL MURAT
              (7,400)

1st Heavy Cav. Div.
  Gen. Nansouty
  Brigs. Piston, de la Houssaye,   1st Carab.R. (Carabinier Regiment)
    Saint-Germain   2nd Carab.R.
                                   2nd Cuir.R. (Cuirassier Regiment)
                                   3rd Cuir.R.
                                   9th Cuir.R.
                                   12th Cuir.R.

2nd Heavy Cav. Div.
  Gen. d'Hautpoul
  Brig. Saint-Sulpice   1st Cuir.R.
                               5th Cuir.R.
                               10th Cuir.R.
                               11th Cuir.R.

2nd Dr. Div.
  Gen. Walther
  Brigs. Sébastiani, Roget, Boussard   3rd Dr.R.
                                       6th Dr.R.

	10th Dr.R.
	11th Dr.R.
	13th Dr.R.
	22nd Dr.R.
Light Cav. Div. Gen. Kellermann Brigs. Frère, Picard	
	2nd Hus.R.
	4th Hus.R.
	5th Hus.R.
	5th C. à C.R.
Light Cav. Bde. Brig. Milhaud	
	22nd C. à C.R.
	16th C. à C.R.

B. THE COMBINED RUSSIAN AND AUSTRIAN ARMY (total losses, where known,
are entered in brackets. Strengths are again v. approximate)

Commander-in-Chief, INFANTRY GENERAL KUTUZOV
Commander of Austrian Contingent, LT.-GEN. JOHANN LIECHTENSTEIN
Commander of First Three Columns, LT.-GEN. BUXHÖWDEN

Advance Guard of 1st Column, LT.-GEN. KIENMAYER
(6,780 and 12 light pieces)

Bde. Maj.-Gen. Carneville	
Broder I.R.	1 bn. 500
1st Székler I.R.	2 bns. 1,300
2nd Székler I.R.	2 bns. 1,300
Pioneers	3 coys. 340
Bde. Maj.-Gens. Stutterheim and Nostitz	
O'Reilly Chevaulégers R.	8 sqs. 900
Merveldt Uhlan R.	¼ sq. 40
Schwarzenberg Uhlan R.	½ sq. 100
Hessen-Homburg Hus.R.	6 sqs. 600
Bde. Maj.-Gen. Moritz Liechtenstein	
Székler Hus.R.	8 sqs. 800
Sysoev Cossack R.	5 sqs. 500
Melentev Cossack R.	5 sqs. 500

1st Column, LT.-GEN. DOKHTUROV
(13,650, 40 light and 24 heavy pieces)

Bde. Maj.-Gen. Lewis	
7th Jg. R. (Jaeger Regiment)	1 bn. 650 (see below)
New Ingermanland I.R.	3 bns. 2,000 (230)
Yaroslav I.R.	3 bns. 2,000 (283)
Bde. Maj.-Gen. Urusov	
Vladimir I.R.	3 bns. 2,000 (238)
Bryansk I.R.	3 bns. 2,000 (463)
Vyatka I.R.	3 bns. 2,000 (229)
Moscow I.R.	3 bns. 1,400 (468)
Kiev Gr.R.	3 bns. 1,000 (70)

| Denisov Cossack R. | $2\frac{1}{2}$ sqs. 250 (4) |
| pioneers | 1 coy. 240 |

2nd Column, LT.-GEN. LANGERON
(11,700, 30 light pieces)

Bde. Maj.-Gen. Olsuvev

8th Jg.R.	2 bns. 1,000 (155)
Viborg I.R.	3 bns. 2,000 (600)
Perm I.R.	3 bns. 2,000 (1,729)
Kursk I.R.	3 bns. 2,000 (1,276)

Bde. Maj.-Gen. Kamensky I

Ryazan I.R.	3 bns. 2,000 (612)
Fanagoria Gr.R.	3 bns. 2,000 (580)
St Petersburg Dr.R.	2 sqs. 200
Isayev Cossack R.	1 sq. 100 (47)
pioneers	1 coy. 150

3rd Column, LT.-GEN. PREBYSHEVSKY
(7,770, 30 light pieces)

Lt.-Gen. Wimpfen, Maj.-Gens. Müller III, Selekhov, Strik, Loshakov, Levitzky

7th Jg.R.	2 bns. 1,250 (801)
8th Jg.R.	1 bn. 500 (155)
Galicia I.R.	3 bns. 1,500 (1,271)
Butyrsk I.R.	3 bns. 2,000 (1,902)
Podolia I.R.	3 bns. 900 (250)
Narva I.R.	3 bns. 2,000 (1,600)
Azov I.R.	3 bns. 700 (498)
pioneers	1 coy. 170 (140)

4th Column, LT.-GENS. MILORADOVICH AND KOLLOWRATH
(23,900, 52 light and 24 heavy pieces)

Advance Guard Lt.-Col. Monakhtin

Novgorod I.R.	2 bns. 1,330 (97 sic)
Apsheron I.R.	1 bn. 500 (see below)
Erzherzog Johann Dr.R.	2 sqs. 125

Bde. Maj.-Gens. Wodniansky, Berg, Repninsky

Novgorod I.R.	1 bn. 670 (see above)
Apsheron I.R.	2 bns. 1,000 (199)
Little Russia Gr.R.	3 bns. 1,500 (274)
Smolensk I.R.	3 bns. 1,500 (253)

Bde. Maj.-Gen. Rottermund

Salzburg I.R.	6 bns. 3,000
Kaunitz I.R.	1 bn. 900
Auersperg I.R.	1 bn. 600

Bde. Maj.-Gen. Jurczik

Kaiser I.R.	1 bn. 1,000
Czartoryski I.R.	1 bn. 600
Reuss-Graitz I.R.	1 bn. 600
Württemberg I.R.	1 bn. 500
Beaulieu I.R.	1 bn. 500

Kerpen I.R.	1 bn. 700
Lindenau I.R.	1 bn. 400
Vienna Jaeger	2 coys. 300
pioneers	2 coys. 340

5th Column, LT.-GEN. JOHANN LIECHTENSTEIN
(5,375, 24 light pieces)

Lt.-Gen. Hohenlohe	
Bde. Maj.-Gen. Caramelli	
Nassau Cuir.R.	6 sqs. 300
Lothringen Cuir.R.	6 sqs. 300
Bde. Maj.-Gen. Weber	
Kaiser Cuir.R.	8 sqs. 500
Bde. Lt.-Gens. Essen II, Gladkov	
Grand Dk. Constantine	10 sqs. 1,000
Uhlan R.	
Gordeev Cossack R.	5 sqs. 500 (33)
Isayev Cossack R.	4 sqs. 400 (see above)
Denisov Cossack R.	2½ sqs. 250 (4)
Bde. Gen.-Adj. Uvarov	
Chernigov Dr.R.	5 sqs. 500 (102)
Kharkov Dr.R.	5 sqs. 500 (108)
Elisabetgrad Hus.R.	10 sqs. 1,000 (134)

Advance Guard, LT.-GEN. BAGRATION
(13,700, 42 pieces)

Maj.-Gens. of Cavalry Voropaitzki, Chaplits, Wittgenstein,
Maj.-Gens. of Infantry Dolgoruky, Markov, Kamensky II, Engelhardt,
Ulanius

5th Jg.R.	3 bns. 2,000 (168)
6th Jg.R.	3 bns. 1,800 (163)
Arkhangelgorod I.R.	3 bns. 2,000 (1,631)
Old Ingermanland I.R.	3 bns. 2,400 (1,099)
Pskov I.R.	3 bns. 2,000 (553)
Empress Cuir.R.	5 sqs. 500 (107)
Tver Dr.R.	5 sqs. 500 (410)
St Petersburg Dr.R.	3 sqs. 300 (48)
Pavlograd Hus.R.	10 sqs. 1,000 (246)
Mariupol Hus.R.	10 sqs. 1,000 (155)
Kiselev Cossack R.	5 sqs. 500 (55)
Malakhov Cossack R.	5 sqs. 500 (4)
Khaznenkov Cossack R.	5 sqs. 500 (25)

Reserve, Russian Imperial Guard, GRAND DUKE CONSTANTINE
(10,530, 40 pieces)

Lt.-Gen. of Cavalry Kologrivov, Lt.-Gen. of Infantry Maliutin, Maj.-Gens. of
Cavalry Depreradovich II, Jankovich, Maj.-Gens. of Infantry Depreradovich I,
Lobanov

Izmailovsky Lifegd.R.	2 bns. 1,000
Semenovsky Lifegd.R.	2 bns. 1,400
Preobrazhensky Lifegd.R.	2 bns. 1,500

Guard Jg.Bn.	1 bn. 530
Guard Gr.R. (in reserve)	3 bns. 2,300
Chevalier Garde Cuir.R.	5 sqs. 800
Gardes du Corps Cuir.R.	5 sqs. 1,000
Lifegd. Hus.R.	5 sqs. 800
Lifegd. Cossack R.	2 sqs. 300
pioneers	1 coy. 100

INDEX

CHARACTERS

Rottermund, Major-General,
brigade commander 4th Column,
117, 183
Roustam, servant, 139

Saint-Cyr, Sergeant-Major, 136
Saint-Hilaire, G., General,
commander 1st Div., IV Corps,
116-7, 119, 138, 140-2, 180
Savary, R., General, 21, 76, 79,
89, 154, 161
Schmidt, Lieutenant-General, 61,
73
Schulmeister, C., spy, 21, 27
Schwarzenberg, C. P., Lieutenant-
General, 49
Sébastiani, H., Brigadier, brigade
commander 2nd Dragoon Div.,
129, 181
Ségur, P. H., aide-de-camp, 50,
89, 122, 145
Selekhov, Major-General, joint
brigade commander 3rd Column,
67, 143, 183
Sievers, Colonel, 146
Soult, N., Marshal, commander
IV Corps, 12, 14, 41, 70, 76, 77,
92, 102, 106, 117, 138, 149, 151,
180-1
Strik, Major-General, joint brigade
commander of 3rd Column, 61-2,
112, 143, 183
Stutterheim, Major-General,
brigade commander, advance
guard of 1st Column, historian,
158, 165, 178, 182
Suchet, L. C., General, divisional
commander V Corps, 129, 130,
181
Sulima, Colonel, commander
8th *Jaegers*, 145
Suvorov, A. V., Generalissimo, 33

Thiard, aide-de-camp, 89, 139, 178
Thiébault, Brigadier, brigade
commander IV Corps, 114, 116,
117, 142, 143, 161, 180
Toll, C. F., Major, 75, 97, 107,
113, 150, 157, 164, 166
Tolstoy, L. N., novelist, his *War
and Peace*: ix, 56, 165-7

Ulanius, Major-General, joint
brigade commander, advance
guard, 128, 184
Uvarov, F. P., General-Adjutant,
brigade commander 5th Column,
98, 108, 123, 131, 184

Valhubert, J. M., Brigadier,
brigade commander V Corps, 129,
181
Vandamme, D. M., General,
commander 2nd Div., IV Corps,
12, 42, 135, 140-2, 180

Villeneuve, P., Admiral, 10
Volkonsky, R., General-Adjutant,
31, 73, 119

Werneck, General, 48, 50
Weyrother, Major-General, staff
officer, 73-5, 78, 93, 95, 103,
117-8; his battle plan, 95-8, 106,
107, 108, 131, 157, 161
Wimpfen, Russian Lieutenant-
General, assistant commander
3rd Column, 75, 112, 144, 183
Wimpfen, Austrian Colonel, 114
Wintzingerode, General-Adjutant,
31, 66
Wylie, J., physician, 116, 121, 150

Zocchi, Captain, 133

PLACES AND EVENTS

Albeck, action, 11 Oct, 1805, 48
Amstetten, action, 5 Nov, 1805,
58-9
Augsburg, 47, 54

Austerlitz:
French forces: 87-8; French
plans, 88-92; allied forces, 92-3;
allied plans, 93-9; terrain, 84-7;

The Battle of Austerlitz was the first and perhaps the greatest victory of Napoleon's *Grande Armée.* Through the graphic recreation of that day in Tolstoy's *War and Peace,* the main features of the action and the characters of the chief participants have long been familiar to generations of readers. What has hitherto been lacking has been a comprehensive and objective study of the battle. Earlier books have tended to concentrate exclusively on the achievements of the French and to ignore the viewpoint of the vanquished.

In this book Christopher Duffy sets out to redress the balance, basing his work on original manuscripts in Austrian and British archives, as well as on recently-published Russian documentation. It includes an assessment of the French, Russian, and Austrian armies, a description of the preceding campaign, and a set of orders of battle.

In general, the book follows the same pattern as the author's widely acclaimed study of the Battle of Borodino. His new book maintains the same high standard of scholarship and readability.